SOUL
BENEFICIARY

THE GOOD, BETTER,
BEST GUIDE TO
Success
— IN —
SELLING INSURANCE

JESSI PARK

ISBN: 978-1-956464-07-8

Table of Contents

Dedication

This book is dedicated to my sister, Jennifer Park Bossenberry, who died from cancer 11 days after her 35th birthday, far too soon. You advised me to venture outside of my comfort zone and try something new during our last conversation, so when I was approached about writing a book, I said yes instead of no. I love you, miss you, and know that you and your children are safe and loved.

Jalen and Jorian, my two children. For what seems like my entire existence, it's just been the three of us. I've tried to make you proud of me and give you a life that I didn't have. I absolutely love you and am so proud of the wonderful humans you've become.

Soul Beneficiary: The Good, Better, Best Guide to Success in Selling Insurance

By Jessi Park

Introduction

My introduction into the insurance industry wasn't because I wanted to be here; it was out of desperation. I always make the joke that "I was forced into it against my will." No one says they want to grow up and be an insurance agent. I certainly didn't; it was never anything I thought I would ever do.

In August of 2016, I was unexpectedly laid off from my Marketing Manager position at a swanky company in downtown Orlando. Truth be told, I never felt entirely happy working in corporate America and had always had side hustles, but this abrupt termination took me by surprise. My salary at that position was $47,770, and while I wasn't entirely satisfied with that amount, I felt that it was enough to live on until I found my calling. However, I liked my coworkers and was content with the status quo. Alas, I had a comfort zone.

So, on that fateful day, when I was called into the conference room and told to pack my belongings and head home, I was devastated. I remember calling my best friend as I drove home crying so forcefully, snot was erupting from my face, and I could barely speak. Weeks prior, she had just joined a captive insurance firm and was optimistic she could arrange an introduction.

During my interview at this captive agency, it was the first time I had ever heard terms like "deductible," and "copay," and "coinsurance." I listened to their sales pitch, learned about residual income, and was instructed to return when I had obtained a health, life, and annuities license. I registered online that night and passed the Florida 2-15 state exam three days later.

I did not last long at that agency because I could not align myself with their values. I did not like the harsh sales tactics, the drug usage in the office, and the general "Wolf of Wall Street" atmosphere. I also wasn't any good because I couldn't sell their portfolio of products with a clear conscience. So I floundered about for a month or so, searching for something else, an FMO to call home, and time and time again, I was disappointed with low compensation structures for agents, no career path if you wanted to grow, and most importantly, they all charged for things agents need like contracting, CRM's and leads.

I had four weeks to succeed in this cut-throat industry before I found myself on the brink of losing everything.

By December of 2016, my $250 a week unemployment benefits were near to running out. In the state of Florida, you only get six months, and after five months of providing for two children on that, I had to make something happen fast. Unfortunately, zero job offers had rolled in, so I knew that I wouldn't get another marketing job soon enough. It was win-or-bust by then, and with no savings, my only option was success. I had four weeks to succeed in this cut-throat industry before I found myself on the brink of losing everything.

I began dialing aged leads in January of 2017 and quickly developed a method that worked for me. I finally started making an income, and as luck would have it, I finally received that long-anticipated job offer after four months of making phone sales. That comfort zone security that I had known my whole life and had longed for just a few months prior was mine again. It was a dream job for a national marketing agency, making 80k with full benefits and a 401k.

I knew that the insurance sales industry has much uncertainty, and the insurance industry, in particular, is ruthless, as it has a 92% failure rate.

However, something in my gut told me to turn it down. I remember hanging up the phone after that phone call and questioning whether I had made the right decision. I knew that the insurance sales industry has much uncertainty, and the insurance industry, in particular, is ruthless, as it has a 92% failure rate. So there was no guarantee of what I would make or if I would even make it. Would I be another statistic? Perhaps, but I saw the opportunity there and felt like I *could.*

However, according to *Forbes,* the finance and investments industry is the number one industry globally that makes the most millionaires.

In 2017, my first year as a commission-only insurance sales agent, I made $137,332.47. That was my breakthrough year. That year started off nearing poverty and ended with the highest salary I had ever made in a year. Of course, I don't want to lead this book with flash and money. However, according to *Forbes*, the finance and investments industry is the number one industry globally that makes the most millionaires. Right behind it is technology, followed by manufacturing (Voytko). The reason being is that in insurance, we earn what is called residual income. This means that as long as you keep working every year, you will significantly compound your earnings year after year.

Aside from exceeding any earning possibilities that I've ever had before, I've started my own company, Inspired Insurance Solutions. I drive every day to an office that I own to lead a company that I founded. Achieving this kind of independence and training my agents to succeed as well is a dream come true. I love finding those diamonds in the rough agents and watching their lives change.

While my brokerage continues to expand and I continue to recruit agents, I know that I'm not going to be able to teach every single newcomer out there.

So my hope for this book is that I can help even just one person that I otherwise couldn't have.

I want this to be the book I wish I'd had when I was a young agent. My story isn't more special or important than anyone else's, but it's not typical in this industry. A lot of the successful people here are men from families with money and industry connections.

There are not many people like me, a woman without any family wealth or connections whatsoever. So in that sense, I'm a bit unique.

I grew up in a lower-income family. My parents worked retail and trade jobs their whole life. They did what they could like any parent would, but dinner was a packet of ramen noodles on many occasions, and we frequently shopped at second-hand stores. When I was a teenager, things got rougher when my parents divorced, and through no fault of my own, I was with nowhere to call home at the age of 17.

Having to find your way at such a young age changes you. It makes you hungry for success.

Having to find your way at such a young age changes you. It makes you hungry for success. You develop a keen sense of survival and an unwavering attitude of gratefulness even for the small things. I remember thinking that I would be happy sleeping in a closet and eating a full meal.

At that time, college was not an option. Instead, my priorities were working (at McDonald's) and paying for rent and transportation. Unfortunately, these circumstances happen to people so often, and the cycle of poverty is challenging to break. College seems unattainable for so many people because even with financial aid, it's not a priority if you don't have a roof over your head.

So many people get stuck with this poverty mindset. It already seems impassable if you grow up thinking of people with nice things as "them." I remember growing up and hoping I'd get to go to college and work in a tall corporate building wearing suits one day. College was not something my family cared about, so the fact that I even wanted to go was foreign. I knew from a young age I'd have to pay for it myself.

When you grow up like that, there are only a couple of ways to escape the cycle of low paying jobs and government assistance; go to college (debt), try to work your way up, join the military, or like my grandma would tell me, "find yourself a rich man."

The room I was renting was a friend of my long-term boyfriend's mother, she had four sons, and her 23-year-old adult constantly seemed to be staring or leering around, so I mostly stayed in my rented room. Then one night, I awoke with him on top of me, pinning me down. I could smell the alcohol on his breath as he started kissing my chest. I acted fast and somehow convinced him that I liked him as well, but since he had woken me up, I wasn't in the mood, and if he waited until the next day, I would be in the mood then. Finally, he left my room, and I was shaking. I couldn't go back to sleep. I realized that I was in a very unsafe situation. I had no money to leave, but I knew I couldn't stay.

The next day my boyfriend packed up my things. His mom had always told us that I could move in with them under one condition. So that's how I ended up getting married at 18.

He joined the military, and we moved to England; I had my son by 20 and my daughter by 22. When she was four months old, I had grown tired of specific issues in our marriage and moved back to Florida to be near my dad. The military and marriage provided a taste of stability that I craved, so leaving that sense of comfort was extremely difficult for me. In addition, I had no college and limited job experience, and now I have two children to look after.

I'm not telling you this to make you feel sorry for me; rather, I'm trying to give you some context for where I came from. It had a significant influence on who I am today. People frequently use their upbringing or circumstances as an excuse for their lack of success or even trying, and while this is a challenge that not everyone must overcome, you can use what you've learned to your advantage.

After living in a motel for a month, I found a job as an executive assistant to a bigwig CEO and quickly adapted. I became an expert at making coffee to his liking (hot, black, and placed on the lower right-hand corner of his desk with no lid), filing, using Excel, making copies, and honed my typing skills to off-the-chart speediness. While he was picky about his coffee and travel arrangements, this man was the first person to give me a break. I had signed up at the nearby community college and asked if I could get off slightly early on Mondays and Wednesdays, and to my surprise, he said yes.

For the next three years, my schedule was working the nine to five, rushing to pick up my kids before their daycare closed, dropping them off at my dad's or ex-husband's mother's house, going to class, running back to take them home, and put them to bed, study until I couldn't stay awake, and then getting up to do it all over again.

I graduated with honors with my Bachelor's Degree from the University of Central Florida at the age of 29. I was utterly crushed with student loan debt, but I figured that I would quickly pay it all off once I had gotten a job with my new degree. I started applying around.

Ironically, the only job I could get with my degree was the exact same thing that I'd been doing this whole time, an executive assistant to some bigwig CEO: three grueling years and a new pile of debt for a $2.50/hour raise. You don't have to be a math whiz to realize that this equation doesn't compute.

People from my background are sold a lie. We are told that college is the answer and that once we get our degree, so many opportunities will present themselves. We are told it is acceptable to take on loads of high-interest student loan debt because you will be able to pay it off very quickly. But the way the system is set up, you won't. The cost of a college education has increased by 3009% in the last 50 years (DePietro). This is how even those that go to college can get trapped within the poverty cycle by debt from school that they'll never actually get to pay off. It's practically predatory.

We are encouraged to take on debt for school, cars, homes, credit cards. We then build our lives on this feeble stack of cards, and when anything happens, like a downsizing, we lose. We're told that trade jobs, blue-collar jobs, and jobs that don't require a college degree are not conducive to someone that wants to do well in life. Yet, schools drill into our children that they need to know what degree they will pursue by the age of 18.

I have news for you, that isn't the only way. As I previously stated, the insurance and financial industry creates the most millionaires in the world.

However, it is incredibly competitive and cut-throat, and most people fail within their first year. I have developed a training method that you can become part of the 8% if you follow. Some people are comfortable where they are, and that's fine, but this book is especially for those trapped in the poverty cycle and who want to do more.

The fantastic thing about this industry is that it offers the opportunity for people like me to rise without any barriers. Glass ceiling? Not here! There is no other opportunity out there like this. However, new agents need to be careful. Be mindful of your FMO; interview them and ask them what they provide. Are they captive? Do they provide free leads? Get the promotion levels in writing.

You don't need a degree to do this, and you can do this alongside a second job. In addition, you can do this from home while taking care of your children.

This book outlines everything that I've learned in my (so far) five years here: what it takes to get into the industry, the daily grind, the closing tactic that I've developed for sales calls, how to manage the initial success, and how to transition up the ladder. I go over my script, how to land any client and make them a client for life, and the mindset it takes to overcome limiting beliefs and mental blockages.

Now, there's a reason 92% fail. It takes focus, grit, and a shift in mindset.

Now, there's a reason 92% fail. It takes focus, grit, and a shift in mindset. It becomes about the long-term goals rather than immediate income. It's hard work, but if you're up for the challenge, then buckle in.

CHAPTER *One*

The Truth About "Easy Money"

From the outside, this industry looks like "easy money." You need to be incredibly driven or have a pressing "why." You'll likely hear stories of fast money and luxurious trips from any sales presentation you attend. And while it is true, it takes a particular type of "hustle" to achieve that.

The barrier to entry is relatively low; all you need to start selling insurance is a high school diploma, a clean record, and a license. The cost of licensure is about equivalent to the price of one credit hour of college and can be completed in less than a week. You will need to find an accredited online or in-person course, get fingerprinted and pass your state exam with a 70% or higher.

Most people are not prepared for how much work it takes as an independent 1099 to build your book of business. It is nothing like a 9-5 corporate job. Being commission-only, you only get paid when you sell a policy. And to sell a policy, you have to have clients. To have clients, you must be actively generating leads. And to many agents, that comes in the form of dialing all day.

While many people are lured into the industry with promises of huge paychecks, they might not realize the hard work to build residual income. For example, the first company I worked at would recruit by showing weekly paychecks with four or even five digits. That might not be completely dishonest, but it is deceptive. It takes time to start building residual income and takes incredible focus and dedication, which are skills learned over time.

Yes, you can make that kind of money. However, most people who come into the industry will not stay at it long enough to ever see a paycheck like that. Mental burnout cripples most new agents within the first six months. That's where preparing yourself with the right mindset is the most critical factor.

There are so many agencies that promote toxic workplaces as well. It's way more common here than most other industries because, in 1099 agencies, there is no Human Resources department since you are technically not an employee. So most workplace norms and standards of behavior do not exist.

Now, we aren't talking about just the typical office gossip and petty lunch groups here. We're talking about elitist groups of top-performing agents blatantly hazing low performers. Or groups of agents who openly consume illicit performance-enhancing drugs in the office so that they work longer hours and make more calls. Or recruitment mandates in which it is mandatory to recruit people to have access to leads. Or better yet, having felons who can't get a license work under someone else's name.

This was my first experience in an agency. In addition to the culture, I also felt uncomfortable with how the agents represented the products. I had only been there a couple of weeks, and I talked to one of the top producers trying to figure out how he did it. Finally, he confided in me that all he had to do was lie, and once he sold the client, he blocked their number, took the advance, and hoped they never used the plan.

I almost quit entirely. I remember going home feeling super defeated and lost. While they all drove around in foreign cars and wore designer clothes, I could not bring myself to treat clients that way, no matter how desperately I needed the money. If this is what insurance sales is, then I didn't want it.

While that's how many sales companies are, that's not what sales need to be. You do not have to scam people to succeed, and you can find a company that operates in line with your internal values.

I'm not necessarily saying that that company was terrible; they are quite successful. All companies will have dishonest agents. In fact, all professions have dishonest people. All problems aside, everyone there had a killer work ethic, and I learned how to dial and prospect during my three months. However, it wasn't a good fit for me personally. It was a captive agency with only one product, and I knew I needed freedom to help my clients with anything they needed. Eventually, I found an FMO that fit me better.

If you are relatively new to the industry, you'll want to do your homework first. It is imperative that you align yourself from the beginning with a company or a mentor that shares your same values. Join a team that's upfront about the work involved and honest about what you can expect to make both initially and down the line. Stay away from companies that take your future renewal income.

The best thing about this industry is what it can do for you and your family long term.

When you start earning a significant amount of money, don't get swayed into that "fast money" culture of sales. That lifestyle is not sustainable. People who are only focused on making money and blowing it as soon as they get it will burn out sooner or later. The best thing about this industry is what it can do for you and your family long term. So I always say, live on your advances, and bank your renewals.

Don't get me wrong. The money is excellent, and the flash can be fun. Just make sure you spend it wisely. A good business tip would be to save 30% for taxes, invest 30% back into your business, live on 30% and save the rest.

I'm very proud of the fact that I can provide for my family. I remember when I realized I was starting to make money, and my bank account was increasing almost daily. I logged into my NelNet account and paid off my student loans in full. They had been haunting me for over ten years. It was one of the best feelings of my life. The other was when I signed the papers for my first home with my children by my side. The way I grew up is very different from how I've been able to provide for them. They have everything they need, and I'm grateful every single day that I can give it to them.

Money is not the end-all-be-all, but it does empower you to do what you want to. When my sister passed in January of 2021, nobody had the money to pay for her funeral arrangements back home. In a devastating situation, I made sure that she had a beautiful service and the most beautiful headstone. I also promised her to take care of her kids and make sure they have school clothes every year. Before this career, that would have put a substantial financial burden on me. Now, I am not only able to buy them school clothes, but now I can fly them to me, take them to theme parks, take off work and spend time with them.

Having extra money coming in means that I could fulfill my sister's last wishes and ensure that she'll know that they'll be taken care of, now and forever. That's what's important. Anything beyond being able to do what matters is just an empty number on paper.

If you get into this industry with the expectation of fast money, you're not going to be able to push through all that constant initial rejection. It's mind-numbing. Later in the book, we go over an entire mindset overhaul to help you. In addition to the transition into the right mindset, you will also need to *work*.

Before we talk about mindset, I want to ensure you have the fortitude and accurate moral compass. Numerous people come into this industry for the money alone, and they don't understand the whole purpose of this position. An agent helps clients choose the best products and build the best policy that addresses their individual needs. The opportunity here is especially remarkable because it allows those who want it to work for a better life while also providing a valuable service for their clients. That's how it's supposed to be, and that's precisely what many people seem to forget.

Insurance can often seem like this very sterile, by-the-numbers thing. However, that's not how

I see it. Insurance can buy back someone's peace of mind. If someone is suffering from a terminal illness, they can at least have some peace knowing that their policy will take care of their family. As an agent, you are going to run into many situations like this. They can be at their most vulnerable time when you call them. Your job is to help them get that peace of mind they need to make things even marginally better. It's not about the money and flashy lifestyles you see online; it's about people's *lives*.

When the stereotypical slimy sales agent "gets one over" on a client by writing them a less-than-perfect policy to make more money for themselves, they can seriously impact someone's life. A lousy policy could put someone in debt, limit their healthcare options, and worse. It can be devastating.

When most people think of the insurance industry, they think of an agent who will do *that*. Unfortunately, it's entirely common. I won't deny that. Our industry's most prominent "image" is some slimy sales guy screaming ABC (Always Be Closing). Overall, it's incredibly off-putting.

I came into this industry with no sales training whatsoever. While that meant that I had a good deal of learning to do, it also meant that I could learn how to sell for myself. As a result, I avoided being tainted by the aggressive sales tactics that other agents use, which became a huge factor in my success.

Instead of using closing lines every other sentence, I simply have a conversation with my clients. We talk—human to human.

Instead of using closing lines every other sentence, I simply have a conversation with my clients. We talk—human to human. Instead of writing policies that make me the most money, I write policies that give the most value to my clients. By injecting humanity in sales and doing what is morally right, I have been blessed tenfold. It's a different way of doing things that I want to bring to a wider consciousness in the industry. But, it all starts with the right people.

There's no perfect type of person that should get into this. A successful mortgage broker or a different kind of sales agent isn't going to do well here magically simply because of their background. The people that I want to work with me are the people that want to work. I don't look for a specific experience or education. I simply look for the hungry ones.

I have a story for this. It's about an interview that my then-assistant set up. She had booked them but didn't properly screen them, and I was already frustrated with her. A few months prior to this, she took my credit card without my permission and filled up her gas tank, and then lied to me about it. I also found out that she spent most of her day filming TikToks in the office. I knew I should have let her go for that immediately, but I also felt sorry for her as she was a single mom and swore it would never happen again. So I stewed between resentment and pity for her.

Well, she hadn't screened any applicants before calling them into the office for an interview like she was supposed to. There were two men; one was sitting across my desk, while the other was on Zoom from his home in Atlanta, Georgia. The man in the office was slouching in his chair with legs spread open and his hand on his crotch. He had noticeably long fingernails that he didn't bother to trim and a stench that filled the room. I'm always rooting for the underdog, though, so I proceeded with the overview. As I talked to him, he just stared at me blankly. It was like I was speaking another language.

I continued with my presentation, but I started getting fed up with his lack of attention. I finally stopped and asked him point-blank if he was even listening to me.

"Yeah," he mumbled.

"What are you looking for?" I asked him, "Seriously, why are you even here?"

He looked confused. He was here for a job, so I figured he cared about making money. So I clarified, "Okay, if you could have *any* salary in the world. What would you want to make?"

"Uh, I don't know," he said, "I guess like $13 an hour?"

I don't know why, but this infuriated me. My assistant, who stole from me, couldn't be bothered to screen applicants and let this disrespectful guy come in and waste my time. So I quickly ended the interview and shut the iPad closed. I didn't even realize the guy from Atlanta was still on Zoom and could hear everything I was saying.

Now, please believe me when I say that I do not usually talk to people like this. I've mitigated many stressful situations over the years and have never spoken this way. However, I am "argument avoidant," and I let everything fester until I am fed up. I had put up with my assistant for a long time just because I felt uneasy about firing a fellow single mom (who also knew and took advantage of that fact). It takes a lot to push me over the edge. For some reason, though, this did it that day.

"What the fuck was that?" I said as that guy walked out the door. "What did this guy possibly say over the phone that made you think he would be a good candidate?"

She had no answer. I went back into my office, absolutely fuming. But, little did I know, the Zoom call never ended. That guy had heard the whole thing. He called my assistant right away and told her, "I want to work for her. I heard the fire in her voice, and I know exactly what she's looking for."

That was on a Friday. He was so sure that he drove from Atlanta to interview with me in Orlando that Monday morning. When I sat down to talk to him, I could hear the quiver in his voice and see his hands shake. His resume listed all of his restaurant experience—a cook, an executive chef, even running his own restaurant for several years. None of that can speak toward an aptitude in sales. Yet, judging just on paper, I never would have hired him.

But like anybody else, I can be wrong. I initially wrote this guy off as a quick burnout, someone who didn't realize what he was getting into. I told him that and thanked him for coming in.

"Listen," he said, "I'll do whatever it takes. Seriously."

So many prospective agents, while they are in an interview, don't close the sale. They don't ask for the job. This guy did. So I decided to give him a chance to prove that he was really up for it.

"All right," I said, "if you can get your license by the end of this week, then you've got the job. I'll even reimburse you for your test and buy your first five states. But if you can't do that, then I wish you nothing but the best."

I sent him on his way and forgot all about it within the day. It's not hard to get a license, but it's not some overnight thing. It's a 60-hour course, and you have to pass an exam. I completed mine in four days, so I thought I would give him five. I know exactly how much work it is to manage it that quickly. If he could do that, then he would be able to do everything else that follows.

Friday comes around, and I'm in my office. He walked with the paper in hand and with tears in his eyes. His name is Aaron, and he still works with me today. He closed one of the quickest first sales I've ever seen, and he continues to crush it.

That moment was pivotal in my career. Aaron changed the way I look for new agents; I had become hardened due to so many people promising work ethic or that they would succeed, only for it to end with them giving up. Before this, I previously favored licensed agents; however, having a license doesn't make a good agent. Grit does. Determination does. Mindset. Their WHY. Aaron had enough of it to drive from Atlanta to ask for a job face-to-face from a woman that he heard yelling over a video call. Now I don't know if that's necessarily a good reason to, but that's grit. He wanted it bad enough that he did everything he could to get it. Someone who has to succeed at any effort is going to succeed here.

People that possess that kind of drive will not get deterred when they hear "no" day after day. They have to want to make the sale more than they want to make money, at least initially. Then, they'll be able to push through until they get that first critical "yes," and then it's only up from there.

On the other hand, those who are only focused on how much they can make and how fast they can make it are probably not going to make any at all. They let themselves get defeated very early on and leave before they can reach that breakthrough. Usually, they are looking for that quick yes, instead of realizing that it will take time to build a book of business. If it were easy, everyone would do it. Unfortunately, many people are also expecting a cushy job. They think that it can't be that hard to sell something that people need. When they realize that it actually takes learning some incredible speaking skills and spending many hours dialing leads, they're out of the game, too.

The bottom line is that the industry is a grind that few people are prepared for the amount of work it takes.

The bottom line is that the industry is a grind that few people are prepared for the amount of work it takes. If 100 people enter the industry today, 92 of them will be gone within six months. These are the statistics. It's a revolving door of people coming in, realizing it's too much work and leaving.

In the next chapter, we'll discuss precisely what to expect in the first few months, how to manage the workload, and how to persevere and become one of the 8% that succeed.

CHAPTER *Two*

Mindset

One of the primary reasons why so many incoming agents fail simply comes down to having the wrong mindset for the industry. As an independent agent, you must transform your mindset from that of a 9-5 mindset to that of an entrepreneur. Too many people believe that the work stops at the end of "office hours" and find ways to blame other circumstances for their eventual failure. And, most of the time, they don't even realize that they're doing it.

If you can identify the flaws in your current way of thinking and take action to correct them, you will be light years ahead of the majority of other new agents.

Shifting your mindset is the key to success. If you can identify the flaws in your current way of thinking and take action to correct them, you will be light years ahead of the majority of other new agents. Although we'll discuss the fundamentals of a mindset shift in this chapter, I strongly encourage you to also purchase my companion workbook, which goes into much greater detail and includes some really useful tear-out sheets for daily reference. The first step to shifting your mindset is acknowledging that you have limiting beliefs and listing exactly what they are. A limiting belief is a particular "truth" or conviction that you believe to be true and thus limits you in some way.

We frequently have these limiting beliefs because we are subconsciously afraid of failure, and so these beliefs will hold us back from even trying. All your life, you've undoubtedly had some self-sabotaging ideas running through your head. Think back to when you were in school. Were there any subjects that were harder for you than others? When something like, say, understanding math doesn't come as naturally to someone as it does for others, that person may just say, "Oh, I'm just not good at math."

Because they are uncomfortable with not being naturally able in this area, they simply write it off as a subject out of their skillset and never improve. These students merely muddle through and never learn nearly as much as their peers when it comes to math. By internalizing this idea that they simply aren't good at math, they stand in their own way of ever getting better and prevent themselves from ever-improving their math skills.

What if that person just needed a little extra help in geometry and would have aced calculus? If they had decided to apply themselves and work a little more complicatedly, maybe they could've even become a mathematician. The concept is the same here. So many new agents hold themselves back from excelling in the industry because they, consciously or not, shy away from the self-improvement they need to do.

Examples of limiting beliefs:

"I'm terrible at talking to people."

"All the carriers and products are too much for me to remember."

"I'll never make good money."

We may deliberately or unconsciously tell ourselves these limiting thoughts. Either way, these beliefs often lead to a self-fulfilling prophecy of failure because we are too afraid to improve our own capabilities and end up never actually doing it. In these circumstances, people will often blame their own failure on these circumstances supposedly outside of their control rather than taking personal accountability.

When you decide to own up to your limiting beliefs and fully commit to achieving success, you open yourself up to the possibility of failing without any excuse. That is unquestionably a bit scary; I get it. But if you're not willing to own up to it and actually try, you are never going to succeed. If you want to give yourself the best chance of making it in the industry, you have to address the limiting beliefs that have put you in this corner to begin with.

Limiting beliefs can also extend to our situations rather than our abilities. I've heard new agents blame their failure on having children or other obligations that keep them from dialing. Believe me, I've been there too, and it truly is possible to do it all. By reframing the things you tell yourself, you can overcome them.

Once you understand that these "true" things are simply limiting beliefs, you can quickly write out what exactly those limiting beliefs are and then rephrase them into a positive affirmation.

"I'm not good at talking to leads." → *"People are going to love to talk to me."*

"I can't learn all these different carriers and products." → "It may take time, but I will learn everything my agency offers."

"I'll never make good money." → "I am going to kill it in this industry."

By addressing what you feel is holding you back and turning it into something encouraging, you can shift from a fixed to a growth mindset. A fixed mindset is one held back by limiting beliefs, while a growth mindset is one where you acknowledge those limiting beliefs and actively work to overcome them. To succeed in this industry, you absolutely need to adopt a growth mindset.

Your growth mindset should also be holistic. It can't be just about your profession; it has to be everything about you. First, you need to address all limiting beliefs and bad habits in all areas of your life, especially when it comes to your health. Taking care of yourself both mentally and physically is the key to longevity in this industry. Next, envision where you want to be in the next few years. Again, this needs to be a complete (and realistic) vision that encompasses all aspects of your life, not just what you want to be making. Write this out in as much detail as possible.

For example:

"Next year, I will make six figures, get a new Jeep, enroll my son in private school, and go to Europe with my partner."

Once you've established what you want your life to look like in the long term, work backward to break down these big goals into small, actionable measures to complete each day.

You've got to speak all of this as if it's true and then go live it. Setting these intentions is pointless without goals. Once you've established what you want your life to look like in the long term, work backward to break down these big goals into small, actionable measures to complete each day.

Shifting your mindset is a matter of recognizing that you have limiting beliefs, reframing them, envisioning your success, setting goals both large and small, and then taking accountability to meet them. And while blockages do exist and are valid, you have to work to overcome them to create a new mindset of growth and success.

With your new mindset, you are ready to take on the initial upfront work to build your book of business and break into the industry. Next, let's talk about the grind.

CHAPTER
Three

The Grind

So, you now know that your insurance sales career isn't going to start sexy. It won't be sexy for a while.

So, you now know that your insurance sales career isn't going to start sexy. It won't be sexy for a while. You understand that you'll have to work extremely hard to get there. But, if you're willing to put in the work and are up for the opportunity, then sit down and get ready. In this chapter, I'll tell you how to set yourself up for success.

You can make this job a little easier for yourself by picking the right agency to work alongside. For some people, having a supportive work environment can be what keeps them working, while somewhere toxic or cliquey might make them quit entirely.

Every agency does things differently, but the way that some agencies operate is downright unscrupulous. Unfortunately, in any industry that offers high rewards for high performance, exploitation will inevitably happen. I've seen agents get exploited from left, right, and every angle that you can think of.

One of the more common types of exploitation that I've seen and that most agents don't even realize is the requirement to pay for leads from your upline. If they don't allow you to use outside sources, they are making a profit from you.

At best, when you buy leads, you're essentially taking a gamble. An agent might buy a lead for $35 and end up making $500 by selling a policy, or they may produce nothing. Many agencies not only charge for leads, but they also require their agents to pay for training and use of their CRM or Customer Relationship Management software. Imagine if you walked into your first day at any other job and were expected to pay for working there. It's egregious.

Many agencies even charge interest on the advances that they give their agents when they sell a policy. So then, they often will have to pay the agency for working. So instead of making money from their efforts, they end up in debt. Especially when so many people come into this industry to work their way out of debt, they can sometimes only accrue more—one agency in particular charges 15% APR on advances.

I've even heard horror stories from other agents that had to turn over their phones to their leaders as part of working there. Their leader would call everyone in their contacts, falsely claim that the agent "referred" them to sell insurance, and not even give that agent a commission if they just so happened to sell a policy. Unfortunately, tactics like this are rampant in the industry, and agency owners and companies often take advantage of the wide-eyed, eager agent ready to invest in their career.

Most agencies are very top-heavy, where C-Level executives are highly compensated, and the agents can never climb above a low-level commission, making them a lifelong hamster in a wheel. I have been extremely fortunate to forge a partnership with my FMO and build my agency. As a result, I can offer my agents free leads, a free CRM, and no interest on advances, and a non-captive opportunity.

Exploitation often goes both ways here. If an agency doesn't treat their agents very well, they are likely not to treat their clients well, either. For example, I left an agency because they pushed us to sell fixed benefit policies. They would get mispositioned as a good thing but written the way that they were, they would often really hurt the client.

A fixed benefit policy is a set monetary payout that your insurance will contribute toward any medical bill. Depending on the amount and the invoice due, it could mean that you would receive a check for the extra coverage at a doctor's appointment or that you may owe the difference.

A fixed benefit should always be positioned as a supplemental plan. Supplemental plans, also known as ancillary plans, should be sold alongside a plan that has a stop-loss, also known as a deductible. Without a stop-loss or max-out-of-pocket, someone can end up owing hundreds of thousands of dollars for a simple hospital visit. This debt can ruin someone's life. According to the American Public Health Association, an estimated 530,000 families turn to bankruptcy each year because of medical issues and bills (Konish). This is why it is so vital that you sell policies to your client that will protect them.

Like I've said, you don't have to scam to succeed here. You don't have to *be* scammed, either. You can help your clients find the best plan possible and make money at the same time. The easiest way to do that is to avoid a captive agency.

A captive agency employs captive agents. Captive agents, also just called "agents," can usually sell only one suite of products but it's always what their agency tells them to sell. Since they can only make money with their products, they may not do what is always best for the client.

Their sales tactics are often very misleading. For example, sometimes they'll claim to represent other products to get the client's trust. They'll even complete price comparisons with other products, but their policy is somehow always going to be less. And that's because they're mispositioning their product with a comparison that isn't equal.

For example, say that they're showing a client their monthly payments on their product versus the Affordable Care Act. What you're supposed to do is calculate the estimated subsidies based on the client's income. But, instead, what they do is completely neglect that. They'll instead show the total amount prior to subsidies. So, the client will think that the monthly payment on a different plan is much more than it actually is. That's just one of the ways that a captive agent can deceive a client into buying their product, even if that's not really the best one for them.

Non-captive agents are referred to as brokers because we can sell any plan on the market. It's the difference between having "A Plan for Everyone" or having to turn clients away.

Since a broker is contracted with every product, they will make money no matter what. Of course, some products might have a higher commission than others, but a broker doesn't have any genuine vested interest in getting their client to buy any specific plan. As a result, a broker is a lot more motivated to sell a plan that's ultimately best for the client, which would mean getting referrals and renewals.

I sleep very well at night knowing that all of my clients are on good products that I stand behind. I will always do right by my clients, even if that means advising them to buy a non-commissionable product. I sell honestly, and I've taught my agents to do the same. That's not exactly common, however.

So many agencies recruit, train, and encourage their agents to use the most misleading and deceptive sales tactics possible.

Scamming people is not a shortcut to success. You might get many people to buy an inferior product, but you might also see most of them cancel that policy when they figure out what they purchased. And you definitely won't build lasting, long-term client relationships. I have clients from when I first began. I have clients that have recommended me to their friends and family. You can't keep clients long-term by ripping them off. We call that "burn and churn" in the industry, and so many agents conduct business that way.

Selling ethically is the best way to do business, and the best way to sell ethically is to be a broker. If you feel comfortable with what you're selling and would truly buy the products yourself, then you're way more likely to stick with it.

You absolutely are your own boss. But if you're not careful with time management and staying motivated, then you can end up being your worst enemy.

Not all agencies are equal, but all agencies are entirely different from a standard 9 to 5. Nobody is going to tell you when to work and what your paycheck will be. Here, you set your hours and determine how much you're going to make. You absolutely are your own boss. But if you're not careful with time management and staying motivated, then you can end up being your worst enemy.

The majority of your time, in the beginning, is spent dialing. Dialing is the monotonous process of calling up your leads. Your leads come from people interested in getting insurance and have given their information to be contacted. They aren't immediately going to buy, however. One-call closes are incredibly rare.

Some leads are old and have already gotten their policies and may get annoyed at being called again. Some people won't answer. Some people will send you to voicemail. The process can be grueling, tedious, and discouraging. It can be a really boring thing to do day in and day out. I have a mindhack in the companion workbook that helps you get through this and makes dialing slightly more tolerable.

If you're new to the industry, you are no one's offspring, and have no connections, then this is how you have to start and build your book of business. Your book of business is all of your clients and their contact information. These are the people that get their insurance from you and refer others to do the same. Building your book of business is critical to success.

That's what the initial grind is all about, and that's why so many people get burnt out so quickly.

If you don't come in with that pre-built book of clients, the only way to succeed is to sit down and call people to build it. That's what the initial grind is all about, and that's why so many people get burnt out so quickly.

Working from home sounds exceptionally enticing to the people who've had to show up somewhere every day physically. But if you're working from home, especially for the first time, then time management can become a genuine hurdle. Honestly, I struggled with that when I started. I'd spent the last decade tied to a desk, so I wasn't used to setting my own schedule.

In the beginning, I found myself procrastinating and getting distracted from dialing. Finally, I would wake up on time and get hyped to get to work. But then I'd get hungry. Since my kitchen was right there, I always figured that I might as well have breakfast before I started making calls. I had to fuel up, right? So I'd cook something real quick.

I'd take my breakfast into the living room. I'd always end up flipping on the TV while I ate. I might as well watch something while I'm sitting here, right? I'd finish breakfast, wash the dishes, and get ready to get down to work. I'd go back into the living room to turn the TV off, but then *The Price is Right* would be starting. And I love *The Price is Right*. So then I'd decide that I can just watch this one show and then get to work. So I'd sit back down.

During commercial breaks, I tried to be productive. First, I'd pop in a load of laundry. But then the laundry wouldn't be done by the time the show ended, and *Let's Make a Deal* would start. And that show is even more exciting. So I'd figure that I may as well watch that one too and wait for the laundry to finish. After that, though, I'd start working.

By the time the clothes were dry, and I'd folded and put them away, it'd be the afternoon. I'd be hungry again. A quick lunch, and then I'd *really* start working...

There's nobody to tell you what to do, and it takes an incredible amount of self-discipline to make yourself productive without any distractions.

I'm not the only one who would do that. I've heard of plenty of other people repeating that exact same scenario every single day. Your mind is really good at tricking you out of actually doing the work. Being in your own environment can often give you plenty of excuses to procrastinate. There's nobody to tell you what to do, and it takes an incredible amount of self-discipline to make yourself productive without any distractions.

That's where the time block chart comes in. I always give this to my new agents and tell them to write down everything they need to do in a day. Of course, working from home gives you the freedom to do all of that, but you have to schedule in between the actual work. Otherwise, those little side tasks will end up taking over your entire day.

So if you have to take your kids to school, or go to a doctor's appointment, or get groceries, or *whatever*, you can block it in here. The time block sheet holds you accountable for getting your work done the same way a boss would. This method is how I manage myself, and this is exactly how I train my agents to manage themselves.

You're not going to get anywhere if you don't dial. And it's arduous, absolutely. It's time spent on tons of initial rejection. It can get especially discouraging to get turned down constantly. But 95% of this business is possessing the mental fortitude to keep pushing. Later in the book, I speak more on this, and in my companion workbook, I have numerous exercises to help you map out your success and breakthrough these barriers and mental blockages.

I'm not going to sugarcoat anything. If you call 400 people a day, you might end up talking to 15. After talking to those 15, about 5 of them will want you to send over some quotes. Out of those 5, *maybe* 1 will purchase from you. However, that one sale might equal $1000 in commission. Once you start making sales, you'll be able to afford higher quality exclusive leads, which will enable you not to have to call as many and have a higher closing ratio. Over time, you'll then start to get referrals and won't need to dial anymore. However, as I said, this takes time.

Every day is different, too. For example, you might get 30 people on the phone one day and 0 the next. Or, you could take the time to send quotes out to 10 people, and then none of them will actually want it. Or, you may get lucky, and all of them want to buy with you.

The real key to staying motivated is to keep your long-term goals always at the front of your mind.

Pushing past these mental blocks and hurdles is a matter of your mindset. The real key to staying motivated is to keep your long-term goals always at the front of your mind.

I like to teach this to my agents by working backward with them. I start with their big goal for the year—if it's getting a new car, enrolling their kid in private school, taking a vacation, or a desired yearly salary, etcetera. Then, we work out how much money they'd need to make this year to do that. Next, we break it down into how much they need to sell each week to hit that target, and finally, we convert that number to how many applications they need and how many leads they need to dial per day, and the hours they need work per week.

When you see how the work you do each day feeds into your big goal in the future, it becomes much easier to sit down and do it.

That's where it clicks for so many people, and they realize that what they're doing now will eventually build into a career that will provide long-term financial security. When you see how the work you do each day feeds into your big goal in the future, it becomes much easier to sit down and do it.

Again, many of the highly successful people are not self-made. I am constantly asked what my secret is. There is no secret. The only secret

I can offer is consistency. If you consistently do something, you will see consistent results. It's getting up every morning and choosing to do it. It's sticking with it even when you're discouraged, and it is understanding that even these seemingly unproductive days will eventually pay off.

The truth is, I still pinch myself. This is so far and beyond what I had ever imagined for my life. I've been told that I'm lucky. I'm fortunate, but I'm not lucky. I worked hard for everything that I have. As Thomas Jefferson is credited with saying, "I'm a great believer in luck, and I find that the harder I work, the more luck I seem to have" ("Jefferson Quotes").[1]

A "no" today doesn't mean it'll be a "no" tomorrow. A lot of those people who initially turned you down may call you back at some point. Their life circumstances can change suddenly. They might get married, have a kid, lose their job, or have other random events that cause them to need new insurance. If you did your due diligence to build a rapport with them and keep that line of

---

[1] The Thomas Jefferson Foundation states that the earliest print appearance of this quote was by Ralph Emerson Waldo Emerson, though Thomas Jefferson may have said it prior.

communication open, then you're going to be the first person they call.

Everyone has the same amount of time. After I figured out how to manage mine, my days started to get drastically more productive. And long, honestly, but I was motivated to make that breakthrough. Once I knew how to keep myself on track, I became a beast.

I would get up at 6 am, get ready for the day, take both of my kids to their separate schools, and then be at my desk by 9 am at the latest. I'd call people in my time zone until about 2 pm, stopping only to pick my kids up from school. After that, I'd do the standard mom stuff—help with homework, make dinner, all that—and then be back on the phones by 6 pm. I'd dial the states on the West Coast until midnight (i.e. 9 pm PST, the latest that you can legally call), take a shower, sleep, and then I'd be up at 6 am the next day.

So every day, I had to decide to spend my time in a way that would pay off.

This schedule was incredibly grueling. It would be for anyone. I wasn't working like this because I preferred it. Would I have instead wanted to watch *The Price is Right*? Of course. But that wouldn't have gotten me where I am today. So every day, I had to decide to spend my time in a way that would pay off.

It took about four weeks of dialing 400 people a day without any pay until I finally made a sale. Once you make a sale, you get an advance. This amount is calculated based on the commission percentage of the product. If you are in an agency that gives advances, this amount is multiplied by the number of months you elect. Most agencies offer six or nine-month advances.

Most agents need advances when they start. Eventually, you'll begin to make renewals on top of those advances. You get paid renewals when a client keeps a policy past the length of the advance. A renewal is a small commission from their monthly payments. It might not be much from one client, but they add up with each client you get. That is how agents start to accumulate long-term wealth.

But if a client cancels their policy before the advance is up, then you'll get a chargeback. So basically, you'll owe the remainder of the advance.

When chargebacks happen, it is disheartening but remember to keep your eye on the long-term goal. If you work each day with a consistent mindset of creating a sales pipeline, you will eventually build one.

Choosing insurance is a significant decision that people need time to make. Someone you talk to today might not call you back for weeks or even months. The first few months are so exhausting because agents often feel like wasted work. You have to have the patience and the persistence to stick it out and see all of those people be ready to say "yes."

In the next chapter, we'll go through ethical sales strategies that get your clients to "yes" a little bit quicker, as well as the Good, Better, Best sales method and script.

CHAPTER *Four*

Dialing

Dialing leads is a straightforward process—you pick up the phone, call your leads, and try to sell them insurance. However, it's the *selling* part that can get tricky. How do you, a stranger over the phone, get someone to trust you enough to help them make a significant purchasing decision?

Many people initially lack the confidence to do this. Remember, if you're working with a reputable agency, these leads *want* to be contacted. They *want* insurance. It's a matter of building enough rapport to get them to buy it from you.

The very first step to this is to pick, at most, three carriers you want to represent. Next, you need to learn the policies, how they work, exclusions, limitations, and how they change based on different factors. The more you know, the more quickly you adapt (and sell!) to the client's needs.

I start training my agents with a script. So many people feel like they need a script to succeed, but I'm afraid I have to disagree with that. A script is a great way to get started and work your way to being comfortable on the phone, but it can often become a crutch. If you're reading off of a script on every call, it's going to be a detriment to your sales, as you'll end up sounding robotic and not genuine.

The flow is the natural rhythm of conversation between you and your client that builds rapport and trust.

Sooner or later, every agent has to stop relying on the script. People don't respond to a mechanical repetition of some pitch and selling points. People respond to other people. So you will need to eventually figure out how to inject humanity into your sales script and be someone they can talk to and trust. The script is only a loose line of questions that you can use to speak to them, rather than a line-by-line recitation to follow. However, there is a flow that you'll need to learn. The flow is the natural rhythm of conversation between you and your client that builds rapport and trust. It isn't regimented. Work on your tonal inflection on certain words and phrases in each of the segments, and make it your own.

Your opener is the most important part of the call. You need to be quick and to the point. Skip the pleasantries and end the sentence with an open-ended question, make them think on their toes, and don't give them an easy way out with a simple yes or no question. There is a strategy behind using an open-ended question as the very first line. You only have about five seconds to catch their attention, so you want to grab it as quickly and efficiently as possible. An open-ended question gets them to talk to you.

Opener: *Hi, is John there? This is Jessi from Inspired Insurance Solutions; I was calling about the inquiry you made regarding your health insurance; is this for you or for you and your family?"*

Next, you want to qualify yourself. Inject something in the sentence to make you stand apart from the other 30 agents calling them. Specify that you are a broker with access to many plans and are simply calling to help them pick out a plan.

Qualify Yourself: *"Okay, perfect. I'm a broker and have access to hundreds of plans. I specialize in helping my clients find plans that fit their needs and budget. I need to ask you a couple of questions so I can see which direction to take this. Okay?"*

Now take out your **Intake Form** or Questionnaire, and be personable as you go through the questions. Don't make it seem like a sterile quiz. Talk to them while you do it.

Questions (Intake Form: *"Now, Sandra, I hate to ask a lady this, but what is your height and weight? Do you smoke?"*)

If they say no, then say something funny like, "Good for you!" Go down the intake form in a conversational manner, talking them through each question.

Next is the budgeting question. This is important because you want to know if the client you are about to go diligently comb through quotes for has a reasonable expectation or if you need to reset their expectations.

Budgeting: *"Okay, John, the last question, so I'm sure you're aware, but there are hundreds of plans. Depending on the way I build this plan for you, it could range in price drastically. So what is a budget you feel comfortable spending each month on health insurance?"*

Finally, you're going to reassure them. Ideally, you will get right to work with your client while they remain on the phone and go into your Good, Better, Best presentation. However, new agents may need to get off the phone to find a plan and call them back and present the plans in the Good, Better, Best method. Whichever way you proceed, a simple reassurance goes a long way.

Reassure Them: *"Okay, perfect. So what I'm going to do now is go comparison shopping and show you some different plans that would work for your situation. I just need you to be able to tell me no or that you don't like something. Okay?"*

(In this last sentence, be sure to change your tone. Make it slightly lower and calmer.)

While you are talking to them, be sure to ask them open-ended questions. That's how you get to know your clients. Ensure you are listening more than you are talking. Also, *during* your conversation, you should be trying to find their **pain point**. A pain point is a client's central issue. It's usually either frustration with their care, fear of not having enough coverage, price, or sometimes something else. The pain point is what they need to address with the insurance package you provide, and that's what you're coming in to fix for them with the right product and policy. Be sure to occasionally repeat their pain point back to them as you present the plans.

<u>For example:</u>

> *"Now, Debra, I know you had said you were tired of not having your doctors in-network; well, this plan has ALL of them in-network."*

<u>Or you could say:</u>

> *"John, I know your family is your greatest priority; this plan comes with a rider that will pay out $__,___ should you suffer from cancer, heart attack, or stroke."*

Each category of insurance addresses different pain points, and each product fills different needs. So to find their pain point and figure out the best product for them, you need to ask them open-ended questions that go through their potential needs.

Examples for health insurance:

- *"Are there any specialists that you see?"*
- *"Are there any doctors that you'd like to keep in your network?"*
- *"How often do you go to the doctor?"*
- *"Do you have any medications that you have to take regularly?"*
- *"Do you travel? If so, how often?"*

Examples for life insurance:

- *"What is your plan to make sure that your kids are taken care of if something happens to you?"*
- *"How would your family manage the debt that you would leave behind?"*
- *"How many months could your family survive without your income?"*
- *"Would your children have to sacrifice going to college or other things if you weren't around?"*
- *"What do you have in place to make sure that you leave behind something for your family and your legacy isn't debt?"*
- *"Since you still have a mortgage, what is your plan to make sure that your family wouldn't have to move if you passed away?"*

Examples for auto insurance:

- *"Who is your current insurance company and how long have you been insured with them?"*
- *"What are your current coverage limits?"*
- *"Have you had any accidents or tickets in the last 5 years?"*

Examples of home insurance:

- *Who is your current insurance company and expiration date?*
- *What is the year built & square footage?*
- *(If the home is older than 15 years.) "When was your roof, AC and water heater last replaced?"*
- *(If the home is older than 20 years.) "What type of plumbing and electrical units is it and has it been updated?" (Request a 4-point inspection.)*
- *"Have you filed a home insurance claim in the last 7 years"*

Each insurance category has a different Needs Analysis, so your line of questioning will slightly vary based on what kind of insurance they're requiring. However, their answers all come together to paint an overall picture of their situation and why they need insurance. From there, you should be able to pinpoint exactly *what* they need and present it to them.

Quick review: The Needs Analysis is conducted by asking open-ended questions to find their pain point. Your job is to find the best products that best address this pain point.

That's why knowing all of the products is so important. If you only know the products that pay the highest commission, you won't be able to figure out what's truly best for them. The product with the highest commission is not always going to fill your client's needs.

That high-paying product might not even be something that your client wants or can afford. Some agents are essentially one-trick ponies. They know one high-paying product exceptionally well and will only present that to clients. If a client doesn't want that product, then they lose the sale entirely. These agents make themselves captive by ignorance and leave money on the table.

You would want to be sold insurance that's best for you, and you would like to buy it from a *person*. If you can ask your potential client the questions on a person-to-person level rather than robotically going through a list, then you'll be able to build rapport with them and establish the trust needed to make the sale. Another aspect of this might not be as "teachable," and that's empathy.

People fear getting sick, dying, losing their homes, and all of those other terrible things that no one wants to acknowledge. While insurance won't stop those things from happening, insurance can ensure that policyholders and their families have peace of mind.

Empathy skills encompass everything that deals with the emotional side of selling insurance. Insurance is what can ease a deep, personal fear for so many people. People fear getting sick, dying, losing their homes, and all of those other terrible things that no one wants to acknowledge. While insurance won't stop those things from happening, insurance can ensure that policyholders and their families have peace of mind.

You want your potential client to feel like they know you. People like to do business with people they like, know, and trust. Especially since insurance often involves them sharing some quite personal, sometimes even vulnerable, information, they need to feel like they connect with you on a human level to do that. So, be conversational. Make appropriate jokes. I love to make my clients laugh.

They need to feel like they know you, but they also need to feel like you're looking out for their best interests. You can accomplish this by reminding them that you are there to provide the best options for them. That's the absolute truth, too. Any good agent wants to *help* their clients. That's what I train my agents to do, and that's what I'm outlining in this book.

Once you have figured out what is best for your client, you can now prepare them for your presentation.

"I've got a couple of plans to look through and compare. But before we start, do you feel comfortable telling me if any of these don't work for you? If they don't, I can always get back to work and find something else."

Make sure you let your clients know that it's okay for them to tell you no. Setting that expectation up prior to your presentation will save you so many sales, I can assure you.

Ensuring their comfort reinforces that you are working for them, and they will generally be comfortable enough to trust what you present. So when they're ready to start looking at plans, I say something like this:

"All right, would you like to start with the cheapest option or the one that I recommend?"

This is a subliminal way to nudge them toward looking at the best plan. That's also how I start to implement my "Good, Better, Best" method. Additionally, it lets you know if the price was a pain point without disclosing that.

Like I have said, I had no prior training in sales. So this method came about organically. I started by initially learning all the available products and then finding out which carriers I could bundle with other products. From there, I looked at those bundled plans that I would personally want, a plan that had the most protection and value for the client.

I liken The Good, Better, Best Method to shopping for a car. Say you go into a dealership and tell the salesperson that you can afford a $300 monthly payment for a vehicle. They're not necessarily going to first take you to the $300/month car.

They're going to take you to that shiny new Lexus with the sunroof, leather interior, heated seats, Sirius XM radio, twin-turbo engine, and all of the other upgrades. It's a beautiful car, and you love it. But, this car is for $360/month. That's out of your budget, and you tell the salesperson that. They offer to show you something different.

They walk you over to a 2004 Toyota Corolla with manual windows and a cassette player. That's not what you want. Anybody would want the Lexus over the Toyota. When you see precisely what you *could* have, your tight budget becomes a little more flexible.

The first and **Best Plan** that you show them is the Lexus. Or, as I say on the phone:

"The first one that I'm going to show you is what I like to call my preferred package. This is the one that most of my clients go with, and you'll see why..."

Then, I name everything that the Best Plan has and explain the complete coverage that it offers. If it doesn't fit their needs, then I pivot to a different Best Plan. If the Best Plan is too expensive for them, that's when I start to disassemble the plan to something within their budget.

Disassembling is taking away certain parts of the plan until the monthly payment is within what the client can pay monthly. The thing is, most people can afford what they want. Everybody wants (and needs) health insurance. Everybody wants to have as much coverage as possible. So when you start to take off parts of the plan right then and there, they begin to reconsider how much they are willing to spend.

"We can go ahead and take off the dental and vision and see what that does to the premium. Is that something that you'd like to get rid of?"

Of course, the answer is almost always "no." Nobody wants to lose any part of their plan. Typically, people are slightly more comfortable seeing what a higher deductible will do to the monthly payment.

Keep a calculator on hand and *always* reiterate the original price of your Best Plan versus this new Better or Good Plan. The difference in cost will either be affordable, or you may have to create a more basic plan or pivot to a different carrier entirely. Keep in mind, some people have an unreasonable expectation for what health insurance costs in this country. I've had people tell me that they expected to get a complete plan for about *$20 a month*. Unfortunately, people accustomed to free plans or Medicaid are not your ideal clients, and there often isn't much that you can do for those clients except offer them a dental vision, accident, critical illness, or perhaps a telemedicine plan; unless it is Open Enrollment or if they have a Special Enrollment into the ACA.

But for other clients, reiterating the original price might make them realize that they can get the absolute best plan *for just x more per month*. It's a little bit out of their budget, but it's worth it to them. So they'll need to readjust some things in their life. For example, they might have to cut down on how often they go to Starbucks or get takeout. If giving up a weekly frappuccino means that they'll be able to have a fully-loaded health insurance plan, then they are almost always going to make that sacrifice.

It's vital that you give them the courtesy and respect to be quiet while they think about it. But, furthermore, being quiet is also just part of sales—the first one who talks loses.

It's vital that you give them the courtesy and respect to be quiet while they think about it. But, furthermore, being quiet is also just part of sales— the first one who talks loses. So you have to give them the time and ability to mentally readjust what they can afford and allow them to talk themselves into it essentially.

If you talk over them or give too much information, they are going to get frustrated. It may feel awkward to let a bit of a silence fall over the phone, but you have to resist the urge to fill the space with more than they need to hear. All you will do is interrupt their internal dialogue and likely deter the sale.

As I have already said, one-call closes are incredibly rare. You will probably not get them to buy right then and there the first time you call them. They have the quote, and you have them sold on it, but they still need time to think. So be prepared to end the call without a sale. Always remind them to call you if they have any other questions or when they are ready to buy.

Something that I did not consider when I first started dialing was that people *will* call you back. Initially, I had no structure past keeping track of the numbers that I had already called on the list and how many I dialed each day. Then, when leads would call me back, I'd stumble. I had not taken any notes, so I would have to ask who they were if I had quoted them and anything else we had talked about. That is not conducive to making a sale.

Using a notebook and some color-coded tabs that I bought at Staples, I created a system to track how each call went, quotes, and when to call someone back. Once I had a system of organization that made sense to me, my productivity skyrocketed. Every agent should come up with their own method to track calls before they even start dialing.

Having records of the who/what/when of your dialing not only helps you be personal and specific with your leads, but it also helps you remember when to call back and follow up with leads that you have quoted. Don't be too pushy with your follow-up calls, though. If they feel like you are relentlessly pursuing them, they'll get scared off. But on the flip side, they may forget about the quote entirely if you don't get them to commit. It's a delicate balance that you have to manage.

When I was still dialing, I would start each day by looking through all the leads that I had not yet closed. My first calls would be to the ones that had hit the one-week mark. The way that I would check in with them went something like this:

"Hey Mary, this is Jessi. I was just wondering if you had gotten a chance to look over that quote I sent you last week and if you might have any questions for me."

Often, I would get told that they liked the quote but were not ready to sign up just yet. You don't want to let them get off the phone with that soft commitment. They may want that policy, but they may also forget or end up spending the money that they would have used on something else. If you end the call without getting them actually committed to the policy, you stand a good chance of losing the sale. To solidify the deal, I would offer them this:

"Oh, that's perfectly fine. I understand. You may want to consider putting in the application today so we can bind the premium, but we can post-date the policy out a couple of weeks so that way you can plan for it."

Of course, this depends on your agency and the plans you represent. This way, the client gets a guarantee on their monthly payment, and you get them to commit. It's a win-win.

This final conversation is crucial to building trust and a long-term relationship with your client. It goes something like this:

Once you have collected payment and are finishing up with the client, it is time for your **Comfort Close**. This final conversation is crucial to building trust and a long-term relationship with your client. It goes something like this:

"John, before I get off the phone with you, I want you to do something for me. Please write down this

number and save it to your phone. I want you to feel comfortable texting or call me anytime. I'm here to help you find doctors, urgent care, and even help with claims should you need it. I plan to be your agent until you reach age 65 and need Medicare (laugh)."

Once you hang up the phone, text him and tell him to save your number. Most agencies will also have a CRM system to monitor the follow-up. My CRM will send emails to follow up two weeks after the call, wish them a happy birthday, and remind clients when they need to renew their policies. If you've done your due diligence to give them your contact information and keep that line of communication open, they will call you.

Making the sale is not the end of your relationship with your client, nor is it the end of your opportunity to earn commissions. I recommend all agents call their clients about three weeks after their policy starts to ensure they received their cards in the mail and check if they have any other questions for you. This also allows you to do what I like to call "**Super-Sizing**."

I learned this sales tactic at my very first job. Back then, all McDonald's employees were required to give all customers the option to "super-size" their meal. So for about 40 cents extra, you could get a larger fry and drink. It's quite genius; it's a few extra fries and about a cup of extra soda, which is essentially water, multiplied by billions of customers. It was a deal that became the subject of a famous Morgan Spurlock documentary.

I was really uncomfortable asking customers that. It felt so "salesy" to me. I ended up getting written up twice for not doing it. My manager at the time threatened to outright fire me if I ever got caught not offering the super-size option. So I started asking every customer if they wanted to super-size their meal, and I was surprised to see that most would opt to do it.

Little did I know, McDonald's was teaching me how to upsell. People are a lot more open to additional options when they have already made the decision to spend money. To them, they are maximizing the value that they're getting out of the purchase. For you, it's an opportunity to make another commission.

That three-weeks-after call is your time to shine. You can say something similar to this:

"Hello Meredith, it's Jessi from Inspired Insurance Solutions. I was just calling to check that you got your cards from [carrier], if you had any questions, or if there's anything else that I could do..."

When it's appropriate, you can slip this in toward the end of the conversation:

"I'm not sure if you've ever thought about this, but I just wanted to let you know that I also offer [something they didn't get in their plan, other types of insurance that you offer, any other services, etcetera]. So if you are ever considering any additional coverage or [other things mentioned], please give me a call."

Again, this is why it's so important to be a full-service broker. If you only know and push to sell one product, you will lose out on so much other money that's on the table. Having a deep knowledge of everything you can offer and the ability to sell it is a significant factor that distinguishes a mediocre agent from someone who will achieve real success.

You can also open the door to passively building your book of business by asking your clients for referrals.

This call isn't just an opportunity to super-size. You can also open the door to passively building your book of business by asking your clients for referrals. If you've done an excellent job of establishing trust and have genuinely helped your client, they are likely to pass your contact information on to their family and friends.

<u>Making a sale is a matter of:</u>

- Having a complete and thorough knowledge of all of the products that you can offer.
- Hitting your daily dial goals.
- Being personable while conducting the **Needs Analysis** with a lead.
- Establishing trust and rapport.
- Listening closely to find their **Pain Point**.
- Building a plan that best addresses their pain point.

- Using the **Good, Better, Best** method to present plans.
- Staying quiet while they think.

If you are committed to the grind, you will eventually make a sale. If you follow everything that I've outlined, you will build your book of business and find success. This may sound contrary, but having that initial success is definitely one of the most dangerous periods of an agent's career. In the next chapter, we'll talk about what to do once your sales pipeline starts to flow.

CHAPTER *Five*

Complacency with Success

Many of those who come into the industry and have the drive to work until they build up their sales pipeline generally have some external motivation pushing them on. They have what is known as a strong **why**. Typically, they want to make more money. However, once they hit that goal, their drive slowly starts to dwindle.

Now, some people have that internal drive to always work hard. Some people, like me, are never wholly satisfied with what they have done. For others, they begin to get too comfortable with their current success. That comfort is where things start to become dangerous.

The complacency with initial success I so commonly see in this industry comes from a couple of things. One, most people coming into this industry are used to directly trading their time for money. Two, some people have misconceptions regarding how this industry works. And three, people often lose their drive when they already have what they want.

Most other jobs pay based on the hours that you physically showed up and worked. If you're salaried, that biweekly paycheck is still calculated based on time expectations. Since most other jobs pay a set hourly wage, most people have grown accustomed to trading their time for a correlative paycheck. They know they will get paid x amount for working y hours, and those factors do not change. However, they are new to the idea of an uncapped but varying earning capacity and a self-directed schedule.

So, they may not know how to handle it when they see residual earnings coming in even when they possibly didn't work that week. For them, it can almost be like cognitive dissonance. They may think something like, *How am I suddenly getting thousands of dollars even if I have taken a few days off?*

But here is the thing—while you are not getting paid directly for your time spent dialing and selling, your performance and the time you put in as a whole will directly impact what you make. So if you worked hard your first year but then started to slack your second year, you should still be getting your residual income if you were a good agent.

This is especially true when your sales pipeline starts to flow. Your first check may be a healthy four figures, but it may have taken you the last couple of weeks to get to that. Each advance is earned by dialing and speaking with leads and converting those into clients. Renewals can be a continuous source of income, but you had to find that client and build a relationship with them. So when you start making "good money," you must keep in mind that you had to build up to it. The money isn't just magically coming in.

You have to continuously feed your sales pipeline to maintain that momentum.

Some people also misconceive that once they have this money coming in, then they are "done" and no longer need work. I've seen so many agents become complacent after hitting $200,000-$300,000 annually and then, a few years later, wonder what happened when that money stops coming in. That is not how this industry is. You don't just work hard for a year and then get to retire. You have to continuously feed your sales pipeline to maintain that momentum. I always tell my agents they need to keep year one energy throughout their career. So many agents lose their drive to keep working once they start to make their goal income.

You need to be hungry enough to stay on the daily grind and succeed. But, especially when you're "well-fed" on renewals, that hunger can often dissipate.

I see that complacency starts most often when renewals kick in. Nobody ever admits it, but they feel as though they can ease up on their grind once they have this "guaranteed" money coming in every month. Every agent I have ever approached about this has denied it. They always claim to still be working. I think that they might not even realize the slippery slope that they're going down.

They might start by thinking, *Okay, I don't have to work 12 hours a day now that I'm making money.* And that is entirely fair—you risk complete burnout if you are operating at that level constantly. But then that mindset starts to spiral. The hours they work begin to dwindle more and more. Eventually, they come to decide that *Well, I only have to work a few days a week because I know I have this much coming in.* I've even seen people go all the way to, *I don't have to work this week. I'm good.* Even worse, *I can take a few months off.*

If you've ever been on a diet, then you might already be familiar with this type of mindset. Some people might start to incorporate a cheat meal once they've lost a few pounds. And that's part of a healthy balance, of course. But for some people, that cheat meal can turn into an entire cheat day. That can also be fine, but sometimes that cheat day spirals into cheat day*s*, a cheat week until you end up entirely off the diet and back to your original weight.

This is much like how agents come to quit working altogether. So many are so used to getting paid after working a certain amount of time. They know that if they don't work, then they won't get paid. Since they can so clearly see the tradeoff of time and money, they never lose their motivation to work.

This tradeoff is not so defined in sales. Some agents can't see all the work they had put in behind the renewals and are no longer motivated to keep working. They may even justify that since they have money coming in automatically, they just don't *need* to work anymore. I mean, why work at all if you're going to get a check either way, right?

Well, nothing in life is guaranteed. We all know that. Somehow, I think many agents don't take into consideration that renewals are not guaranteed either. While renewals can be a great source of steady income, they only last as long as the client. Getting a renewal is absolutely dependent on them continuing to make payments on that policy.

You cannot count on clients to keep and pay a policy forever and ever. Circumstances in their lives can change in the blink of an eye. They could lose their job, move, get married, or even pass away. Whatever happens, they might cancel their policy at any point in time.

It doesn't matter how happy someone might be with their policy. Most of the time, it has nothing to do with that. Clients are inevitably going to cancel policies, and you are inevitably going to lose those renewals. If you are not actively working to continue building your book of business or service your existing clients, then your income will eventually dissipate.

I have seen it happen plenty of times. Agents can't grasp the long-term consequences of living solely on renewals and end up losing everything they had worked for in the first place. I have often also seen this issue compounded by agents going wild with their money once it comes in.

Some agents, especially those who have never really had money before, don't know how to handle this sudden influx of income. They are not used to having anything left over after paying their bills, so they spend all their money as soon as they get it. I've noticed agents, especially young men, buying things they have coveted as part of the "rich" lifestyle— Gucci belts, leased BMWs, designer shoes, and other extravagant purchases. They don't put any money aside, which seriously hurts them if they have any unexpected expenses or stop working.

Every agent needs to put away at least a quarter of what they're making so they can pay their taxes when the time comes (I also recommend filing as an S-Corp Limited Liability Company, so you aren't "double-taxed," but talk to an accountant about that). After that, you must consider what long-term benefits money can bring over the short-term thrill of finally having a pair of Prada shoes.

First off, don't spend money on things that depreciate in value. Build up your savings. This is all just fundamental financial advice. The biggest thing is to get the necessities *before* the accessories. Pay off any high-interest debt and get what you need before you make any "fun" purchases. The showy stuff can wait until you have everything else covered.

Keeping a level head and being strategic with your money will help you elevate your overall lifestyle rather than just a few flashy trinkets.

I believe that this industry is not where you can "get rich," but where you can acquire wealth. There's a huge difference. Keeping a level head and being strategic with your money will help you elevate your overall lifestyle rather than just a few flashy trinkets. While it can be challenging to adjust out of the mindset of the direct time-for-pay, it's critical to understand that you have to keep putting in the effort to get new clients because you are eventually going to lose some of the ones that you have now. If you want to keep making money, then you have to keep working. It's that simple.

That doesn't mean you need to work as hard as you did when you started. If that's not personally sustainable, you do not have to continue putting in 60-80 hours a week. But, again, you can ease up on the grind in a balanced way that doesn't devolve into not working at all.

The key is to keep yourself accountable. If you want to only work 35 hours a week instead of 60, by all means, go for it. But just like when you started dialing, you need to block that time out and stick to it. So, for example, if you decide that you're only going to work from 9 am-3 pm on weekdays, you need to make sure that you actually sit down and pick up the phone during that time.

And you need to *always* answer when a current client calls—check in on your existing client base by sending out occasional emails. Taking care of your clients isn't just good business practice; it can also help you get referrals. Referrals are how you can passively build your book of business and cut down on your overall working time. But you have to keep your clients happy enough and ask them to recommend you.

By sticking to your hours and ensuring client satisfaction, you guarantee the checks will keep coming in. While income can fluctuate significantly in this industry, you can generally even come to see how much you need to work to make what you want.

Your earning capacity truly is uncapped here, but that can be enough for some people. There's a certain number they are satisfied with, and they'll work just enough to maintain that and nothing more. They might not ever make much more than what they are right now, but they probably also will never have to work any more diligently than they do. They don't mind being stagnant. Some people are okay with being okay.

And that's fine. Everybody has different needs and wants. I'm someone that always wants more than what I have. There has never really been a point that I have considered myself "made" in this industry. I am very fortunate to have broken out of the poverty-debt cycle, and I am pleased with everything I've done. However, I also know I have a lot more room to grow. I always want to continue to build on my current successes and keep going. I've tasted scarcity, and that's not anywhere I want to be again. If you only have one goal to reach and maintain after, there's nothing wrong with that. Again, different strokes for different folks.

The fantastic thing about this industry is that *you* are the one to decide what you make.

The fantastic thing about this industry is that *you* are the one to decide what you make. So those who want more and are willing to work for it will continue to see their income increase as they continue the dialing grind: the more clients, the more advances, the more renewals, the more money.

Most agencies will reward agents with a higher percentage commission based on meeting certain milestones in sales. They can do this because while the insurance carrier will pay a specific commission to the agency for every sale they make, the agent does not get the entirety of that commission. Everyone above them gets an override or a cut of it.

Your agency or FMO should be very transparent with who gets what percentage of that commission. Ask to see a "point spread," or a spreadsheet that shows the different levels of everyone who takes a cut of the commission. Overrides are a part of this business, and you shouldn't have any ill feelings about someone getting an override on your work, especially if they provide any level of support; leads, training, office space, education, or team functions.

Most agencies will move you up a level after writing a certain amount in premiums, so you'll eventually even make a higher percentage on what you are selling. However, most agencies are built very top-heavy and have a very narrow point spread. Those agencies have a point of view that producing agents will always be producing agents like a hamster in a wheel, and their commission eventually caps at a certain percentage. This is actually the standard with most FMO's so do your due diligence when selecting one.

Find an FMO that also offers real opportunities for advancement. Talk to them before signing any paperwork about your desires for advancement. For example, do you one day dream of leading a team? Do you hope to become a career agent? A leader or manager is someone that can recruit and build up a team of producing agents under them.

A leader can not only get advances by selling policies and collecting renewals, but they can also receive overrides on any policies that their agents sell and collect renewals on those as well. Take a moment and consider how much money that could be. Being a leader is a fantastic opportunity that most FMO's don't offer, and if they do, the point spread is minimal.

Moving from a producer to a leader can sometimes be tricky to navigate. In the next chapter, we'll cover how to manage that transition upward.

CHAPTER *Six*

Transitioning Up

Before we begin, I do want to clarify a few things. First, the industry is rampant with opportunistic people. Some agencies prey on wide-eyed, eager agents and charge them for everything from contracting to a CRM fee, and fees for typically free things like ACA certifications.

Some people come in and are allowed to advance, while others are charged for leads to go door-knocking. A woman recently came to my agency because she had been working at one for years and had written over $3 million in business, but was still an entry-level agent and had been denied a management position. No matter where you go, opportunistic people are everywhere.

Most new agents don't understand the risk of exploitation and often don't even realize they are being taken advantage of as well. As I've already said, choose your agency, FMO, or manager wisely. Review your contract with a fine-tooth comb prior to signing anything. Don't let yourself become stuck somewhere just because you did not read the terms and conditions.

I had gone through two captive FMOs before I landed at the FMO where I made my career. In my current contract with my FMO, anyone you bring in becomes your agent after you write $1 million in premiums. I hit that $1 million within eight months. While I was a writing agent, I somehow managed to recruit 12 friends and friends of friends.

Reaching that million so quickly and having so many people was extremely rare. Yet, I have been asked so many times, "How did you do it?"

The recipe is simple:

- A pint of work ethic.
- A heaping cup full of setting my intentions.
- A quarter cup of people skills.
- A dash of luck.
- A pinch of being a badass (not giving up when it got tough).

Setting your intentions and goals is extremely important when you first start.

It was also something I had intentionally set out to do. Did you catch that? These were my *intentions*.

Setting your intentions and goals is extremely important when you first start. In my accompanying workbook, I teach you exactly how to do this.

All five ingredients were essential to my quick rise. During my full-time writing agent days, several people reached out to me from the first captive FMO I was at and asked where I had gone. Of course, they soon hopped on board with eager excitement. I also told one of my artist friends about what I was doing. She told her best friend, her best friend told a lady at church, and that lady brought her husband along. It was all essentially a rapid trickle effect just from me answering the casual question, "What are you doing for work?"

By the time I had reached that million in Net Annualized Premium, I had twelve agents who had started working with me. I had unintentionally built up a sizable team for myself in the brief period before I was even a leader. And, honestly, what happened to me in my first year has not happened to me since. Nowadays, I may interview one person out of 30 who will go on to write policies. So, having that many people underneath me as soon as I became a leader is extremely rare. I would not advise anyone to expect they can amass that many top-quality agents that quickly, either.

I knew I would eventually become the leader of all these people and that I had to assert myself as a leader in their eyes. I wanted them to know that not only was I capable of achieving success for myself but that I was capable of leading them to success as well. So, while I was still just a producing agent, I started to preemptively train everyone.

We first met up in the local library, but we got kicked out for being "too noisy." So after that, I had everyone over at my house for training sessions every Friday.

I still dialed every Monday, Tuesday, Wednesday, and Thursday. At this point, I was comfortable enough with my sales that I could dedicate Fridays to training. But clients always take precedence, and if I got a call, I would always tell everyone, "Hey guys, I have to take this." It didn't matter what we were doing. If my phone rang, I would go upstairs and answer.

Oftentimes, they would all huddle in my bedroom office to listen in on the call. They got to hear me talk to a client live, but the priority was always taking care of my client. Even if you are transitioning to a leader, your client always needs to be your number one concern.

I've seen many people make the mistake of not maintaining their book of business in anticipation of overrides. Instead, they think, *Why should I work if I have people making money for me?* Well, that's simply not how it works.

First off, you should never rely on anyone else for your income. A dependency on others not only leaves you in a vulnerable position, but I believe that nobody should ever live solely off their agents' work alone. Doing so can often make a leader "too comfortable," a danger we have already discussed earlier.

Leaders can become complacent on overrides the same way that agents can get complacent on renewals. Like a renewal, an override only lasts as long as that agent does. Though with overrides, the threat of sudden loss is even more dire. If your agent quits or goes somewhere else, every override you made on every policy they ever sold will completely and suddenly vanish. So it's not just losing the residual on one thing; it's losing the residual on *everything*. Depending on how many clients that agent had, this could represent a substantial cut of your monthly income.

Also, recall what I said at the beginning of this book: out of 100 people coming into the industry, maybe eight of them will stay. Out of those eight, maybe one or two will truly become successful. People are fickle, and few will go on to become "profitable" for you. You could recruit and train dozens of people, only to get *nothing* in return. Maintaining the presumption that you are 100% going to get overrides on the people that you recruit and train could lead to losing your pay entirely.

You are ultimately responsible for your own income, and you need to maintain your book of business enough to support yourself.

That is only if you are reliant on those overrides. You are ultimately responsible for your own income, and you need to maintain your book of business enough to support yourself. You cannot allow yourself to fall into the position where your agents are your only income.

Aside from practical financial advice, continuing to actively dial and work alongside your agents will also prevent resentment. The most effective leadership is on the ground. You must practice what you preach. If you aren't in the office with them, your agents may start to feel like you aren't really "with" them at all.

Leaders stop coming to the office the same way agents stop working. They initially only take Friday off, and then Monday, and then eventually they're playing golf all the time. It's not a good look. But, unfortunately, when leaders start depending on their agents and taking them for granted, they often also take advantage of them. I have seen people rise to a leadership position only to turn around and become precisely what is wrong with this industry themselves. I've had agents tell me they haven't heard from their manager in over a year.

Being a leader is also not for everyone. If you cannot put the needs of your team ahead of your own, establish camaraderie, and guide people toward their own success, you should not transition up. There is no shame in that. Some people are not meant to do it. I've seen many great producing agents transition to awful leaders, and they end up getting hated for it.

I attribute much of my success as a leader to the fact that I absolutely love doing it. In fact, I wholeheartedly do feel like I was made to do this. I'm talented at talking to clients and figuring out the best policy for them, sure. But running my agency and leading my team is what gets me out of bed every morning. So that's what I have a genuine love for.

As I transitioned from a producing agent to a leader, I noticed that my "why" for working shifted over time. When I was dialing day in and day out, I was doing it to feed my kids and pay bills. It was a matter of meeting basic survival needs. Once I was no longer on the brink of poverty and debt, my "why" was to provide a better life for my kids. My continued drive to keep building my book of business and my small team supported that.

Now, my kids have everything they could ever want and need. I am blessed not to have to worry about that anymore. That is no longer my "why."

Having my own agency has enabled me to help others in situations like the one I once was in. I love taking people under my wing and showing them how to succeed. This is my new "why."

Like I've said, this is one of the few industries that allows anyone to come in and crush it. Success is based on performance, sustaining your efforts, and consistency. I had the drive to do it. I was also very fortunate to have found a structure that allowed me to work my way up to where I am today. Many agencies don't afford this same opportunity to their people. In my agency, I can give others the opportunity that I was given. I am infinitely grateful that I am in the position to do so.

In any case, I am far from perfect. There have been times where I could have done better or where I did not handle things appropriately. But I do try my best, and my best is to have my team's interests at heart. My agency has grown so tremendously; I had to stretch and grow out of my comfort zone, too. It's been a great learning experience along the way.

My ultimate goal is to *inspire* people (hence the name) and give them all the tools they need to uplift themselves. I try to give everybody every opportunity to succeed. I will do whatever I can for those who want to take this opportunity and are willing to work. If that means buying an agent a license, phone, or laptop so they can work, then I will do that.

Being generous and trusting has not always worked out so well. I have wasted hours coaching people who quit their first week. I have even loaned thousands of dollars to agents who took my money and disappeared. But I've accepted that's more or less just part of the process. Not every person is going to have the same good intentions. So I will inevitably get taken advantage of on occasion.

Still, these few bad instances are worth the many good ones. I've gotten to help countless people learn the skills and gain the confidence needed to absolutely kill it. I have so many agents who are single parents like me, and seeing how their success improves their lives and their children's lives means everything to me.

Their successes compound my success. I do well, and my agency grows when my agents succeed. There is so much money to be made in this industry.

But, unfortunately, money often brings out the most greed in people. Greed can make an otherwise good person do bad things and a bad person even worse. I feel that a lot of the seedy side of the industry has ultimately stemmed from greed.

The thing about the greed in this industry is that many people act with a scarcity mentality. They need to have it *all*. I simply don't understand that. I might have a differing viewpoint, but I see it as that there is plenty for everyone. I operate from an abundance mindset. Stephen Covey initially coined these terms in his best-selling book, *The 7 Habits of Highly Effective People*. There is so much opportunity for people to make so much money; I don't need to worry about taking it all for myself. There is plenty for everyone.

As I work with an abundance mindset, I don't ever feel threatened by my agents' successes. Their achievements don't take anything away from my own. So, there is never any reason to steal, lie, cheat, or try to "get one over" on an agent in any way.

If you treat your people well, I genuinely believe that you will be rewarded tenfold.

I'm all about manifesting positivity and goodness in the world as the way to success. If you treat your people well, I genuinely believe that you will be rewarded tenfold. So beyond reducing your turnover rate, it's about doing the right thing and being blessed for it. I have succeeded to the degree that I have because I train and treat my people right. And I wouldn't have done it any other way.

Because I empower my agents to do well, they do well. And because I don't try to capitalize on their success, they stay and continue to do well at my agency. I work very hard to make them happy, so they rarely leave. I have an army of happy, well-paid agents, and that's worth more than a million that constantly come and go.

So if an agent does decide to go, I wish them well on the journey. It's the cycle of any business owner. You can't make 100% of the people happy 100% of the time. Also, keep in mind that not everyone will like you. Some people hold biases *they* may not even be aware of—maybe they don't like men (or women) leading them, your race, it could be anything. So just know, you can't please everyone. Move on and choose to work with the people who *want* to work with you.

Knowing how to recruit, train, and treat your agents right is critical to prospering as a leader. In the next chapter, we'll talk about getting the right people, showing them how to succeed, and keeping them in your agency.

CHAPTER *Seven*

Leadership

Recruiting is the first step of building up a team. You need to bring people in, train them, and guide them to success. To me, this is the barest outline of how to be a good leader. So, it would be best if you started by finding viable recruits.

As I've said, my first year of incidental recruiting was a giant streak of luck where people came to me. I have never experienced anything like that since. So this one-time case of serendipity was admittedly very advantageous to establish my agency without first going through the recruitment process.

When I began to *actively* recruit, I had my then-assistant post on job sites and schedule interviews with potential candidates. If you can recall the beginning of this book, then you already know that this strategy was not so successful.

Had she followed directions, things may have turned out differently. I had to waste a great deal of time talking to people she could have quickly weeded out with a 30-second phone call. But, I also got one of my strongest agents to date through this, so it all worked out.

Now, I have four full-time employees on staff. They use many different avenues to identify candidates—job boards, job fairs, recruitment platforms, and social media. For other leaders looking to recruit, I would say online would be the best place to start.

There is no secret platform or job board to utilize. My advice is to simply post everywhere you can. Social media can also be quite a helpful tool to get people coming to you since just about everyone in the world is on social media. I, like many other people, personally use Instagram (@jessicristinaah, if you were curious). For the past couple of years, I have done social media drip campaigns. This simply means I talk about my company and the opportunity in a way that feeds people over time, and they become curious and apply. It's soft; fun videos, agents celebrating sales, team members at the office. It's not the harsh, down-your-throat type of recruitment.

You might already be familiar with the slimy sales rep who constantly pitches get-rich-quick schemes and pose with stacks of cash in front of a rented luxury car on a beach or something equally gaudy. I roll my eyes at those kinds of posts. They contribute to that overall detestable image of the industry. But, especially when so many people have lost their incomes due to the pandemic, I find these copious displays of wealth slightly insensitive.

My social media is a reflection of my life, and much of my life revolves around my work. So naturally, my followers know what I do and see that I'm doing well. People can get interested from seeing you succeed online the same way they would from hearing about it in real life. Posting about your success as an agent allows you the opportunity to tell more people than you would have the reach to in the real world.

I try to strike a balance between showcasing the opportunity and not being ostentatious when I post online. This year was the very first time that I ever posted my yearly bonus. I was proud, and sometimes you need to show the monetary potential, but I still cringed when I posted it.

It's essential to show how lucrative this industry is *without* bragging about your own successes. I recommend being honest and not putting up the flashy front that so many other people tend to. If you do it right, your followers will reach out to you directly. There are so many ways to showcase the opportunity without being obnoxious. However, sometimes that shock value works at getting people's attention. Oftentimes, people are so locked in to their day-to-day routine that it takes something shocking to get their attention. So do whatever feels right to you. It's your social media, after all.

When you talk to those people who are potentially interested in joining, be authentic. You shouldn't have to try to slip them any typical sales lines or recite a script. I like to set up a one-on-one Zoom call with a potential recruit, share my screen, show them point spreads, carriers, compensation, bonuses, and opportunities for advancement.

I'm writing this book with the assumption that everyone reading this wants to come into this industry with the intention of succeeding by helping their clients and guiding other agents to do the same. That said, I can only imagine you would genuinely be excited to show people this industry and to uplift them. The more you believe in your own opportunity, the more your passion will rub off on others and get them excited about it.

That genuine happiness and excitement is the key to recruiting, at least in my book (no pun intended). People are naturally going to get excited and *inspired* to join after talking to someone that really "buys what they're selling," so to speak.

That's not to say you should recruit anyone and everyone interested, though. They may be a 1099 agent, but they are still working under you and need to be vetted accordingly. I thoroughly interview and assess all potential candidates before offering them a position in my agency.

The people that succeed the most here are big dreamers, money-motivated, and thrive on the challenge. And that could be anyone.

In this industry, education and work history are irrelevant. The people that succeed the most here are big dreamers, money-motivated, and thrive on the challenge. And that could be anyone. I don't care if someone has been a top real estate agent for the past twenty years or checking receipts at Walmart. A resume will not indicate if someone has the chutzpah to be an agent. The only things that can is their "why" driving them to succeed and their grit to do it.

This is difficult to spot for a few reasons. One, it's rare. Most people do not have the motivation to start or the grindset to sustain, or only have it depending on their current circumstances. I don't think I was even ready for this industry until I got to the point I was at. Someone could have had the right "why" a decade ago or might not have it until next year. It can be incredibly challenging to find someone at the right point in their life. Two, it's all internal. Nobody is going to list those qualities on their resume. So you have to strategically conduct interviews to determine whether or not someone has what it takes.

The most basic qualifications to check for are that they can speak to someone and use a computer. I have tried to work with people who weren't articulate or technologically literate in the past, and it never worked out. If they don't know how to talk properly on the phone or turn on a computer (yes, that has actually happened before), then that should probably be an immediate pass.

Beyond that, I have a few other red flags for potential candidates:

- If they know they have their resume out there, but still answer the phone in an overly casual manner. That irks me to no end. I'm not asking everyone to speak like they have a Ph.D., but opening the call with "Sup" or "What?" instead of a simple hello is a terrible way to start.

- If they show up to the interview disheveled or unprepared, that's usually a sign of them now knowing how to manage time. Being proficient in time management is pivotal when dealing with clients and setting your own schedule.

- If they scoff at a commission-only compensation. Granted, I did too at first, but that usually means they will not be able to see the opportunity of an uncapped earning potential when they only care about getting paid directly for their time.

You want to find people who display professionalism, want more, and are open to sales as the means to achieve it. Someone who shows all of that may not necessarily have the "*why*" and grit, though. That's why interviewing people is so important. Every question you ask should be to find out their "why."

While I'm not particularly eager to focus on the money, it is important to ask them what they are looking to make in their first year. If the candidate states a low figure like $30k, which tends to be a common number, that is most likely a red flag. Of course, it could also mean that is their understanding of "good money," but it usually indicates they don't have the drive to work for more than that.

If they can set big goals for themselves, they are typically willing to work as hard as they need to reach them.

You want to find someone with big goals, someone who says, "I'd really love to make six figures." If they can set big goals for themselves, they are typically willing to work as hard as they need to reach them.

Once I explain the earning potential and how much upfront work is required in that first year, I always ask how many hours per week they are willing to work. If the answer is around 20-30 hours,

I know they don't have the work ethic I require. I'm looking for the person that says, "You know what? If 80 hours a week is what it takes to build my book of business, then I'll do it." That shows me they know what they want in the long-term and understand what they'll need to do to attain it. *That's* who you want on your team.

Ultimately, you should be able to trust your intuition to determine whether someone is suitable to recruit. So long as you don't make judgments based on their education or previous employment and instead focus on how they present themselves to you at the moment, you will often make the correct decision.

The right person is never going to be a perfect agent right off the bat. However, training is the make-or-break factor for *all* agents' success and retention on your team, and it's one of your most significant responsibilities as a leader.

I begin my training with every new agent by sitting them down and having what I call a "Welcome Aboard" session. In this session, I keep things simple:

1. I go through the basics of dialing, our CRM, and two of our major carriers out of the 200+ available.

2. I compare and contrast these two carriers and then show them how to build plans using the Good, Better, Best Method.

3. Once they feel comfortable with the basics and these two carriers, I get them on the phone.

These baby steps are one of the core reasons behind my team's success. People can only take so much at a time. They will absorb infinitely more through an incremental learning process rather than get overwhelmed with information about *every* carrier and product available.

Learning everything about everything before they start dialing can cause what I call "paralysis by analysis," where an agent will delay doing the actual work by choosing to stay in that learning stage rather than getting on the phone. They don't need to be the absolute expert before they can start. My agents only need to know how to build the most typical plans with the two most commonly used carriers to begin dialing. At that early stage, any information beyond this is only going to distract them.

I've had several people reach out to tell me how they struggled with information overload during their training at other agencies. Other agencies often try to teach everything at once, and I've heard many complaints that it "all ran together," and they became overwhelmed with everything they tried to learn. What this means is that when you try to teach everything, they learn *nothing*.

I teach them more carriers and products as questions and unique cases pop up. Learning on the go allows them to be productive and put their knowledge actively into practice. The more calls they make, the more they come across, the more they learn.

Some new agents are uncomfortable with the idea of jumping right in with only the essentials. It makes them feel too vulnerable when so much is still unknown. While it's easy to understand their fears, it is your responsibility to assuage them and nudge them forward in the process. Whenever I have a new agent who seems unsure about starting without knowing everything, I ask them three questions.

1. "Do you trust me?"
2. "Do you believe that I am training you to be successful?"
3. "Do you think I got to where I'm at by following these steps?"

The answer needs to be, and always is, a hard "yes." They must have confidence in your leadership, and so you must build rapport with your new agents as you would with a client to get them to trust your guidance. You will not lead your agents to success any other way. If your agents don't have faith in you, then you have nothing.

By streamlining their training and getting them on the phones as quickly as possible, you also significantly increase your chance of retention. Think about it—most people are coming into this industry because they need income, and quickly. They may not have weeks to spend in unpaid training. So I initially only teach my new agents what they absolutely need to know to start the grind sooner, get paid faster, and learn while they are doing it. This is imperative to retention.

They joined your team because they believed in the opportunity. They believed in you. To stay, they must see for themselves that the opportunity does indeed exist. The whole goal is to show them the money in their account and affirm that this is all real. Once they get their first checks, it becomes tangible. The sooner this happens, the more confidence they build in themselves as an agent and the more likely they will stay for the long term. The key to keeping people at your agency is succinct with the initial training and quickly getting them on the job.

Recruiting only those with an internal drive to achieve will drastically reduce the number of agents who quit too soon. Still, it can be difficult for even those with a "why" to get through the challenging period of building up the sales pipeline. So, I do a one-on-one session with my new agents to write down their big goals. Then, I show them how to break it down into what they need to do each day to achieve those goals. They are much more likely to stay motivated when they can keep that big picture in sight and know how every day on the grind will get them there.

Building camaraderie is also essential for boosting motivation and overall morale. Many agents need support not just from their leader but from their associates as well. While there are many ways to peel an orange here, I'll explain what I have personally done to establish a "team spirit" in the office.

I created a group chat for everyone on my team. Agents can ask sales questions, share achievements, and other related communication. As soon as an agent becomes contracted, I add them to our chat to get acclimated to everyone. Your new agents must become familiar with the team early on. Knowing who the other agents are and feeling like a part of the family often makes the job feel more "real" for them and cements what they are doing.

Another thing I do is coordinate team outings. It's a great way to get your agents to connect face-to-face and spend time together in a fun setting. When I first started my team, I did not have the money to take everyone out. Money doesn't determine whether you can do this. You can scale your outings based on your budget.

I started with small gestures that I could afford. For example, on some days, I would offer to take anyone that showed up to the office to a nearby bar after work and buy them a shot. I would also host White Elephant parties during the holidays, which are inexpensive since everyone brings a gift. Little things like these can go a long way when your agents see that you're putting in the effort to get everyone together and show your appreciation for their work.

When someone really feels like they are a part of the team, they are a lot less likely to leave it.

I've since been able to host more extensive outings as the agency's success has grown. I very much enjoy throwing huge parties and going out with my team. We've gone to places like Top Golf and Dave and Buster's and eaten at ritzy restaurants like Seasons 52 and Del Frisco's Double Eagle Steakhouse. But no matter where you take them or what you do, what matters is that you facilitate bonding and a team spirit. Camaraderie is one of the biggest keys to retention. When someone really feels like they are a part of the team, they are a lot less likely to leave it.

Leading a team and keeping people happy often requires the empathy to understand and manage the many nuances of every agent. No agent will be exactly alike, so you must take the time to sit down and get to know them. This is quite similar to what you do to learn and take care of your clients' needs.

Dale Carnegie's book, *How to Win Friends and Influence People*, spoke on nine hallmarks of great leaders. As the book is almost a hundred years old, I've outlined the hallmarks he spoke of in more modern terms below.

Carnegie's 9 Hallmarks of a Great Leader

- <u>Praise them genuinely.</u> If someone is doing something well, tell them! Make sure every member of your team knows how much you appreciate their work.

- <u>Don't criticize them directly.</u> If you call them out head-on, they may respond combatively.

- <u>Admit your faults before pointing out theirs.</u> This takes people off the defense and keeps you from looking like a hypocrite.

- <u>Frame your commands as questions.</u> The best way to get someone to do something is to make them think it was their idea. Lead them there with strategic questions.

- <u>Acknowledge their improvements.</u> By letting them know when they are doing better, they'll feel like their efforts are validated and will continue.

- <u>Set the assumption that they are amazing, and they will become amazing.</u> You'll give them a lot to live up to and motivate them to meet it.

- <u>Cheer them on.</u> Encouragement from a leader is critical to a team's success.

- <u>Present their faults as easily fixable.</u> If it seems too difficult to solve, they will often get discouraged and give up. By making the solution seem simple, they will be motivated to do it.

- <u>Make them happy to do what you ask.</u> Your directives as the leader should be presented as a win-win for everyone.

Taking care of your agents means knowing their motivations and affirming their achievements through reward communication. Reward communication is much like the various love languages or the ways in which people show and perceive affection for one another. Here, reward communication refers to the ways that appreciation for hard work can be displayed and perceived.

Reward communication typically comes in one of three ways:

- Monetary (such as a bonus or cash prize)
- Recognition (praise, promotion, public acknowledgement)
- Gifts

Like the love languages, there's no one-size-fits-all approach. Some agents need validation more than others, and so recognition is the best means of doing so. Other agents may value going out with their family, so gift certificates to different restaurants are what they'll appreciate the most. Your agents all have different motivations, so it's up to you to tailor and adjust your reward communication based on the individual.

A considerable breakthrough I have made in my leadership is realizing that most agents will want a combination of all three. I try to incorporate all three into my leadership skills and lean on a specific one depending on the person. Knowing what to use and when to use it takes a great deal of intuition and understanding of your agents, which might not be something that can be taught. Again, not everyone is necessarily cut out to be a leader. Some people have a natural aptitude that others do not, and that's completely fine.

Even a natural-born leader can't avoid the occasional complacent agent. Unfortunately, as I've said, it is that common. However, there are a few things that you can do to keep your agents from resting on their laurels.

The best way to generally prevent this is to run contests or create incentives that drive people to continue working, even if only on a short-term basis. Sometimes, people can become re-motivated by a more immediate goal to keep working towards than the larger one. Weekly or monthly sales prizes are the easiest way to do this.

If an agent is becoming complacent, you can always sit down with them and talk about it. Let me restate here that I have never, ever had an agent openly admit to getting complacent. Most often, people will vehemently deny it and even get defensive. You may not want to take a direct approach to this, as it likely will not be a successful confrontation.

Instead, I approach it in a more gentle manner. Rather than outright saying that I think they are getting complacent, I take out the list of goals they had written when they had started. Then, I'll ask them, "Did you accomplish all of these yet?" They most likely haven't. Pointing this out may be enough to get them recommitted to achieving them. If they have reached all their goals, you can always suggest writing new ones.

Ultimately, you cannot be motivated for someone else. If your agent becomes complacent and stops working, there is not much you can do about it. Therefore, it is imperative that you find intrinsically motivated people and create an office culture that makes them want to come to work. All you can do on your end is to be a good leader.

Being a good leader ultimately comes down to recruiting the right people, training the right people with an incremental learning process, fostering camaraderie amongst your agents, and having the skills to manage your agents based on their individual needs. This all takes time, effort, and a bit of natural intuition to achieve. It's not for everyone, either. There exist great agents who would make terrible leaders.

Succeeding long-term does not always mean eventually establishing a team. People can build prosperous and lasting careers without advancing into that position. The key to continued success for *everyone* is the ability to pivot. In the next chapter, we'll talk about this last skill every agent needs to succeed in this ever-changing industry.

CHAPTER *Eight*

Staying Sharp

Let's review: it takes drive, grit, and work to succeed in this industry. When you achieve initial success, you must avoid becoming complacent to continue to do well. But to stay successful now, tomorrow, and each day after that, you have to adapt gracefully.

I know I'm saying this as someone some people could consider a "novice" within the industry. After all, I haven't been doing this for as long as many others. But I have seen what those who are continuously successful have done year after year—adapt. I am constantly in the process of adapting. I will always be so that I am never unprepared for when it comes time to change.

This industry truly is survival of the fittest. It has a natural way of weeding out those without grit and longevity in mind.

This industry truly is survival of the fittest. It has a natural way of weeding out those without grit and longevity in mind. Unless you came in with a pre-built book of business, only those who can work hard will make it. We've more than covered that.

Motivation and work ethic is always a given. The biggest key to your long-term success is having the ability to change when necessary.

As with everything else, insurance is in a constant state of change. The differentiating factor here is that the insurance industry is also heavily regulated by current politics. As a result, insurance is a major platform issue. Every candidate runs with a different stance, and we're never quite sure what each politician will do. What we're doing now can completely change based on the election's outcome, and it can change *fast*.

Many agents can become distracted by all the money they are making at the moment. They often forget the ever-changing nature of the industry in which they work. These abrupt changes can feel like getting the ground ripped out underneath your feet if you aren't prepared to pivot. The easiest way to stay ready for these changes is to never get too rigid with your way of doing things. Just as you can't get too comfortable with what you're currently making, you also can't get too complacent with what you currently know.

In 2017, the law briefly changed to limit private health insurance to only a three-month term. While avoiding any political commentary, this three-month limit was not exactly helpful whatsoever for clients who needed private insurance or for agents writing those policies. Clients couldn't renew their policies if anything happened during those three months, and agents couldn't make money because such short-term policies don't pay much at all. It was a bad situation all around.

This was just one of many wrenches thrown at us, and we always need to learn how to overcome it. My team and I came together to figure out how to best help clients with this new regulation and pivoted to selling bundles that fit their needs. Most agents understood these bundles and adapted to the change, but I had an older agent who just couldn't do it. He continued to sell these three-month policies. Eventually, he ended up quitting.

It's very unfortunate, but it goes to show the danger of being unable to adapt. If you can't learn to work with whatever is currently happening, you will eventually get left behind. That's the brutal truth of it.

The thing about change is that it's constant. Oftentimes the laws and regulations that make our jobs a little more complicated right *now* don't stay that way forever. Under the Trump administration, these three-month limits eventually expanded to three-year plans by 2018. Sometimes it can also take having the moxie and mental fortitude to tough it out when new laws make things difficult.

Being able to adapt is just a matter of being open to change, staying sharp, and having faith. This ability isn't always a natural thing that someone just has internally. But, sometimes, it can be learned.

You can't allow yourself to get too rigid in your "way" of doing things. That's also why it's so important to be a non-captive agent or a one-trick pony who only knows how to sell one product— confining yourself to only one type of product places all your eggs in one basket. The first step of being *able* to change is being *willing* to do it. And that's all on you.

When you are continually working to grow as an agent, you never get too stuck to what you are currently doing, and your capacity for change increases every day.

The most successful agents constantly improve their skills and learn new and different products to incorporate into their skillset. When you are continually working to grow as an agent, you never get too stuck to what you are currently doing, and your capacity for change increases every day. Staying sharp is a major determining factor for longevity in the industry.

Faith is critical as well. You had to have faith in the opportunity to come into the industry, and you need to have faith to stay in this industry. Remember that this is a necessity-driven industry independent from the economy. People are always going to need insurance. So, there is *always* money to be made here. You just have to persist to figure out where.

As an insurance broker, you can pivot to different products when one is no longer profitable. There are a variety of products to be sold. If health insurance dips for whatever reason, then focus on life and annuities. Medicare is another very profitable segment. It's also essential to align yourself with a capable and knowledgeable leader who can help you pivot to these different areas when needed. Again, you must do your due diligence to choose the right agency. When things get difficult for a captive agent or a single skilled specialist, they will not survive.

Politics are entirely out of our control, and it can be frustrating when new external regulations are introduced that cut your ability to make money in the short term. But you have to keep the big picture in mind.

When the going gets tough, the tough get going. You need to have the drive to stay at the top of your game, the flexibility to learn and do new things when it's time to pivot, and the resilience to keep dialing.

Eventually, the market always sorts itself out. Being able to roll with the punches and remembering that things will work out is critical to getting through each and every change in the industry.

Conclusion

If you've made it this far, you've likely committed to jumping into the insurance industry. That's great! Before you do, I have some final practical points for you to consider.

First, I highly recommend any agents to create a Limited Liability Corporation or an LLC. It's relatively inexpensive and easy to do so. You just need to go onto your state's website and pay a yearly fee in order to register for one.

An LLC isn't just recommended for those entering the insurance industry—it's for anyone making money. The reason why people want an LLC is because it limits their liability should something happen. For example, if you get sued, your cash and other assets are usually considered untouchable. Funneling your income through an LLC can also be beneficial from a tax standpoint, as you will generally end up being taxed less.

For the same reason, I recommend filing as an S-corp as well. An LLC taxed as an S-corp means the owner's salary will be a business expense, so they will report salary and other business profit on their personal income tax return. But, the owner will only pay taxes on their own salary (not on Social Security or Medicare). Thus, it essentially prevents you from being "double-taxed." So, forming an LLC and filing as an S-corp is ultimately the best route to go for personal protection and tax purposes.

While I am not an accountant and cannot go into much more detail than that, these are all things that my accountant had recommended to me and that I found beneficial for my business. And though this all might not mean much for an agent just starting out, you will eventually make good money if you work diligently. When you experience that breakthrough and begin to build your wealth, these technical recommendations can help maximize and secure your earnings.

Again, that's all down the road. Right now, all you need to start selling insurance is:

- A license.
- A computer with an Internet connection.

- A phone.
- Pen and paper.

And that's it. Things like the time block sheet and a system of organization will help, but this list of tools is the absolute minimum you need to get started. If you know at least two of your carriers, you're ready to get going.

You don't have to know everything upfront to be a good agent; you just have to be willing to learn on the go and do what's best for the client.

As I have previously said in Chapter 6, I see so many new agents who feel like they need to know everything about everything before they can begin. But there is *so* much to learn. It'll take years of experience to become an absolute expert. Even then, there's always something new to learn. Avoiding *paralysis by analysis* is as simple as recognizing that you will not know everything when you get on the phone, and that's okay. You don't have to know everything upfront to be a good agent; you just have to be willing to learn on the go and do what's best for the client.

The initial anxiety can be intense. It's very common, too. You're coming into a completely new industry, and you will feel a tremendous amount of pressure. You can't possibly know all the answers to every possible question. What if someone asks you something that you don't know? Remember, it's okay not to know. If it ever happens, you can say something like this:

"You know what, Mary? That's an excellent question. I've never been asked that before. I don't know the answer right now, but I'll find out and get back to you."

Do your research, talk to your upline/manager/mentor, and call your client back once you have the answer. This is how you learn. Very few people will take issue with you admitting that you don't have the answer, but most people will see right through it if you try to come up with something on the spot.

You already know more than the client. You are the one who obtained a license and went through training. Your focus on that first call is to gauge whether they are interested in buying insurance and, if so, going through that intake form of questions.

You don't have to worry about the what if's; you just need to focus on your prospective client and listening to their needs. If there's anything that you can't answer, you can always call them back when you find out the answer.

And no matter what, the worst thing that can happen is getting told "no," and that's just inevitable in this industry. Rejection is going to happen. You may even get hung up on or yelled at. So what? You'll have to learn to brush that off. As long as you keep in mind that a lead is a lead is a lead. It's someone who went online and submitted their information. There's no need to overcomplicate or worry too much about all these potential scenarios. All it will do is stress you out and keep you from getting to work.

This is why I start my agents with just two carriers. When they can learn two, then they can learn four, then six, then ten, then twenty, then thirty, then a hundred. You will eventually become a pro, I promise. It just takes time to ease into it and soak up all the knowledge.

You might be a little scared right now, and that's okay. Any opportunity like this can be intimidating at first. Please understand that I mean it when I say:

You will be okay.

You are going to get through this.

You can handle anything that comes your way.

You are going to kill it!

But, you have to push through your initial nerves and get on the phone. Then, all you have to do is work. It can also be terribly daunting to look at the entirety of the goal ahead. So, don't. If it's too overwhelming, just focus on meeting your daily tasks. You can do this if you've broken down your big goals into smaller, more manageable ones. If even 400 calls a day sounds like too much at first, shoot for 100 and see how you feel. You can always work your way up to it.

Again, the companion workbook is incredibly handy for new agents to gain confidence and stay motivated as they manage the initial grind.

Again, the companion workbook is incredibly handy for new agents to gain confidence and stay motivated as they manage the initial grind. It starts by addressing your mental blockages and limiting beliefs, then works on shifting your mindset, laying out plans and exercises to plan for your future self, and finally giving you tons of tools to create the life you dream of. You can scan the QR code below to access the workbook on Amazon.

You've already been open-minded enough to consider this opportunity and brave enough to actually take it. That's more than what most will ever do. If you've read this book, you're already ahead of most other people entering the industry. Now, all you have to do is get to it.

Though I've already said how only about 8% of new agents will stay in the industry, I truly hope everyone reading this will make the breakthrough, find success, and kick ass. Good luck!

Glossary

Advance: An upfront commission paid to an agent upfront when they sell a policy. The amount is calculated based on the expected commission that would be paid out over a certain period of months (usually 6 months or 9 months).

Ancillary Plan: Also known as a supplementary plan. An additional type of coverage to be sold with a plan rather than by itself.

Binding the Premium: Submitting a client's application now in order to guarantee what their monthly payment will be. This is offered when the client gives a soft commitment and when an agent is able to post-date the policy to when the client can actually start paying it.

Book of Business: The list of an agent's clients and their contact information.

Bonus: An additional monetary payout that an agent can receive based on meeting a sales milestone, goal, or for any other incentivized goal.

Broker: A non-captive agent. They are able to sell their clients a plan with any type of product from any carrier.

Burn and Churn: The practice of scamming a client or otherwise selling them a less-than-perfect plan purely for personal gain. This practice values unethical, short-term gains over building long-term relationships with clients and working in their best interests.

Burnout: When an agent becomes overly exhausted or disappointed with the industry and quits. This happens when a new agent does not have realistic expectations about the workload and pay.

Candidate: Someone who may potentially be suitable to recruit and train up as an agent.

Captive Agent: Also just called "agent," an agent who is only able to sell a limited range of products that their agency offers. Their products may not be what the client really needs.

Caps: The "limit" or highest commission level that an agent can achieve. Top-heavy agencies will have low caps for producing agents.

Carriers: The insurance companies that provide the actual coverage for clients.

Chargeback: When a client cancels their policy before the period of time that the advance was paid out for, the agent will have to pay back the difference. A chargeback can also include interest on the advance, so an agent can end up owing even more money than they were originally given.

Client: Someone who has purchased insurance from an agent or broker.

Comfort Close: When an agent calls a client once their policy begins in order to open the door to a long-term relationship, offer other insurance products, or ask for referrals.

Commission: The payment an agent receives when they sell a policy.

Commission-Only: A compensation structure wherein a worker will only be paid based on sales made. Most agents work on a commission-only basis.

Complacency: When an agent gets too comfortable with what they are currently making and starts to slack off.

Compounding: When one thing builds on another. In this industry, it refers to how an agent's income is compounded by advances and their renewals.

Contract: An agreement between an agent and a client guaranteeing the detailed services for the established price. It can also refer to the employment agreement between an agency and their agency.

Copay: An amount that a policyholder will have to pay for healthcare related services alongside what their insurance will cover.

CRM: An initialism that stands for Client Relationship Management. This is typically a program that an agency will use to email follow-ups and policy renewal reminders. Some agencies will charge their agents for use of their CRM.

Deductible: A set amount of money that a policyholder must pay before their insurance policy will cover claims.

Dialing: The process of calling leads in order to try to create and sell insurance policies.

Disassembling: Taking away certain aspects of the current plan in order to lower the monthly premium. How you turn a Best Plan into a Better Plan, or a Better Plan to a Good Plan.

Drip Campaign: A social media or email campaign that offers "drips" of information to viewers instead of pouring out all of the information in one video. This means releasing information through multiple posts in order to garner interest and build an audience.

Earning Capacity: The amount of money that someone is able to make. In the insurance industry, there is no limit to an agent's earning capacity.

"Fast Money": The misconception that the insurance industry is a quick and easy route to getting rich.

Fixed Benefit: A set monetary payout that your insurance will contribute towards any medical bill. This should be sold as an ancillary plan rather than on its own.

Follow-Up: To call a lead again in order to check in with them, answer any questions, and see if they are looking to buy.

FMO: An initialism that stands for Field Marketing Organization. In insurance, this essentially refers to the umbrella company and structure in which an agency is built under.

Full-Service Broker: A non-captive agent who is well versed in different insurance products and can offer a larger portfolio to clients. They have the potential to make the most out of all producing agents.

Good, Better, Best: Jessi's sales method wherein plans are presented from the highest to lowest. By doing this, clients are able to see the value of a fully-loaded plan and often readjust what they are willing to spend on their health insurance in order to get that.

Grind: The grueling initial work a new agent must do in order to build their book of business.

Incremental Learning: A training method where information is introduced in small chunks that compound.

Information Overload: When a training includes too much information at once, thus resulting in the new agent being unable to retain anything.

Intake Form: The initial questionnaire used by an agent to become familiar with a client's situation and discover their pain point.

Leader: Someone who recruits, trains, and manages a team of producing agents underneath them.

Leads: Prospective clients. Leads are usually people who have already given their information and are interested in purchasing an insurance policy.

License: A type of certification that permits agents to sell insurance.

Limited Liability Corporation: Otherwise known as an LLC. A type of private company that an agent can form in order to protect their assets and reduce their liability.

Manifest: The embodiment of certain qualities, actions, or appearances. Making something happen by shifting one's mindset and working for it.

Milestone: Major sales goals. Achieving certain milestones might mean a promotion to a higher commission level or the opportunity to transition into leadership.

Mindset: A positive outlook of determination and focus that's needed to push through mental blocks and hurdles.

Mispositioning: The practice of purposefully using an inaccurate product comparison in order to make a sale.

Needs Analysis: A line of questioning used by an agent to determine the client's pain point and insurance needs.

Net Annual Premium: In insurance, this refers to the net sum of premiums written by an agent in a year.

One-Trick Pony: A broker who is "captive by ignorance," or only knows how to sell products that pay the highest commission.

One-Call Close: An incredibly rare situation wherein an agent is able to sell a policy to a lead in the first call.

Opener: The first thing an agent should say when dialing. Their opening introduction should be quick and to the point.

Open-Ended Questions: Questions that can't be answered with only a "yes" or "no."

Override: A cut of a commission that a producing agent's leader will receive.

Pain Point: A client's central issue or fear to be addressed through an insurance policy.

Paralysis by Analysis: When an agent will delay doing actual work by remaining in the learning stage rather than getting on the phone. Waiting until they've learned "everything" instead of learning the basics and then the rest through experience.

Pivot: To rapidly change when the situation calls for it.

Point Spread: A spreadsheet that shows the different levels of everyone who takes a cut of the commission.

Policy: The client's chosen insurance plan that the agent has built for them.

Portfolio: All the carriers, products, and plans that an insurance agency can provide for their clients.

Poverty Cycle: This refers to the multiple systems that keep people in a lower socioeconomic class from generation to generation.

Premium: A client's monthly payment for their insurance.

Producing Agent: An agent who actively dials and writes policies.

Product: The various types of insurance available to clients.

Quote: An estimate for the plan's cost.

Recruit: To bring a new agent onto the team.

Referrals: When a current client recommends their agent to someone else.

Renewals: A small monthly commission given to an agent when a client keeps a policy past the length of advance.

Retention: The goal of keeping agents on the team and reducing turnover.

Residual Income: Income that builds over time. In the insurance industry, this means the renewals and overrides that accumulate.

Reward Communication: How a leader can display their appreciation for hard work in a way that an agent will best receive it.

Team: The group of producing agents under a leader.

Team Outings: Group activities or events to foster camaraderie amongst agents.

Time Blocking: A chart available in *Soul Beneficiary Workbook: The Good, Better, Best Companion* to help structure an agent's daily tasks in between work.

Training: A leader's process of teaching new agents how to sell and coaching them through the initial grind.

Transitioning: The period of time when a producing agent becomes a leader.

Turnover: The rate of which agents quit or otherwise leave an agency.

Sales Pipeline: The flow of sales. Once an agent makes their breakthrough, their pipeline is considered "on" and they will start to close leads.

Scarcity Mentality: Thinking that there isn't "enough to go around," thus justifying selfish and greedy actions.

S-Corp: Filing as an S-Corp prevents you from being double-taxed as both an LLC owner and a 1099 entrepreneur.

Script: Prepared lines of dialogue to follow when dialing. Experienced agents rarely use these, as a script can make them sound robotic.

Soft Commitment: When a lead indicates that they'd like to buy the policy, but they aren't ready to right now.

Super-Sizing: Upselling to a client by offering other available services.

Upline: The person who recruited a new agent into the agency.

Walk and Talk Agent: An agent who builds their book of business solely through in-person networking rather than dialing. Considered the "old school" way of selling insurance.

<u>Why:</u> An agent's reason for entering the industry and working. This is their driving force for success. An agent's "why" can change throughout the years.

<u>Year One Energy:</u> The enthusiasm that new agents have and drive needed to sustain the initial grind.

<u>8%:</u> The approximate percentage of people who actually stay and "make it" out of everyone who enters this industry.

<u>1099:</u> A type of employment status wherein those workers are considered independent contractors rather than a recognized employee within the company. Those filed as 1099 workers do not get taxes automatically deducted from their income or receive employee benefits. Sales agents are contracted as 1099 employees.

Acknowledgements

To my parents, thank you for always trying and doing the best you can. You inspire me in ways in which you do not know.

To Joseph Eichman, you have changed the industry and have changed the lives of thousands of people. Thank you for everything.

To Dan Mack, Joe Krivelow, Bill Pauley, and Barry Draper, thank you for being mentors, coaches, and most importantly, my friends.

To my agents, your hard work and dedication impresses me on a daily basis. I feel incredibly blessed to have worked with each and every one of you.

To Milot, my handsome boyfriend
turned fiancé as I wrote this book.
Thank you for your undying support.

To Staci Fitzgerald -
I hired you as an assistant
and you've become my friend.
My right-hand woman
helping me run my business,
I see it. Thank you for your dedication, spirit,
and heart and soul. You are so special to me.

To Nando Miguel, my friend.
Thank you for helping me pick out a book title.
You understood the assignment.

To Mrs. Jessica Revord-Winters, my 12th grade
English teacher. You instilled a love of writing in
me and it wasn't until this book that
I realized how much I forgot it.

References

Carnegie, Dale. *How to Win Friends and Influence People*. Simon & Schuster, 1936.

DePietro, Andrew. "Average Cost of College Has Jumped an Incredible 3,009% in 50 Years." Yahoo! Finance, April 9, 2019. https://finance.yahoo.com/news/average-cost-college-jumped-incredible-122000732.html

"Jefferson Quotes and Family Letters." Monticello. Thomas Jefferson Foundation, 2021. https://www.monticello.org/site/research-and-collections/i-am-great-believer-luckspurious-quotation.

Konish, Lorie. "This is the Real Reason Most Americans File for Bankruptcy." CNBC, February 11, 2019. https://www.cnbc.com/2019/02/11/this-is-the-real-reason-most-americans-file-for-bankruptcy.html.

Voytko, Lisette. "How Billionaires Got So Rich in 2021." *Forbes*, April 8, 2021. https://www.forbes.com/sites/lisettevoytko/2021/04/08/how-billionaires-got-so-rich-in-2021/?sh=3e9fa44b92c0.

To the Reader

Thank you so much for taking the time to read my book. If you found it helpful in any way, I would appreciate it if you could leave a review on Amazon.

If you would like to learn more about my agency, please visit my website below.

https://www.inspiredinsurancesolutions.com/

Again, thank you so much!

About the Author

Jessi Park is an entrepreneur, artist, author, and mother. Prior to starting her own agency, Inspired Insurance Solutions, she was a top-selling agent. She lives with her two children in Central Florida.